Have A Good Report

Christian Credit Repair

Financial Freedom Series, Volume IV

by
John Avanzini
and
Deborah McNaughton

HIS Publishing Company
Hurst, Texas 76053

Have A Good Report
Christian Credit Repair
Financial Freedom Series, Volume IV

ISBN 1-878605-08-9

First printing: 45,000 copies

Unless otherwise indicated, all Scripture quotations are
taken from the *King James Version* of the Bible.

Cover design and illustration by Bob Haddad.

HIS Publishing Company
P. O. Box 1096
Hurst, Texas 76053

Dedicated to all those

who will benefit

from the information herein.

Contents

Important Notice

The information in this book is given in accordance with the statement written below.

This book is intended as an educational tool to provide you with lay advice on ways and means of repairing your credit report and is not intended as a substitute for sound legal and accounting advice from your attorney or financial advisor.

These are procedural suggestions, not specific directions. Before acting on any of these suggestions, you should thoroughly check what has been written to determine the proper course of action you should take.

The information in this book is, to the authors' knowledge, conceptually correct.

If your credit report contains anything that is not in accordance with federal, state, or local laws, or in any other way contains wrong information, neither this publication, its authors, nor its owners will seek remedy for you or provide you with advice concerning relief. In such matters you should contact your accountant or attorney at your own expense.

Introduction

by John Avanzini

With the advent of the Fair Credit Reporting Act of the federal government, the citizens of our nation have received a new power. With that piece of legislation, we have been given certain rights concerning our credit reports. Not only have the masses received power, but limitations have been put upon the power of credit agencies.

Within that act is outlined our legal right to have our credit history properly handled and accurately reported. That act also gives us access to the information contained in our credit reports. Best of all, it gives us the right to refute and correct any discrepancies or inaccurate comments being circulated about us.

For many years I have known that God wanted His people to have a book on proper credit repair. Several years ago I attempted to write such a book. I thoroughly researched the subject. I bought resource materials and even attended a seminar that dealt with the necessary procedures. However, each time I started to write, God quickly rejected everything I tried to bring forth on the subject. The voice of the Holy Spirit would say, "No, not yet."

The Door Opened To Unscrupulous Men

I now know He purposely stopped my earlier attempts because many unscrupulous methods were being

11

encouraged. With all the good accomplished by the Fair Credit Reporting Act, there have also been many uninformed voices speaking as "experts." They have misled many, even counseling some to lie and perjure themselves. Those are deceptive practices unfit for the children of God to use. Christians must avoid such untruthfulness at all costs, for we, of all people, are to be examples of righteousness.

A Proper Book For God's People

Not until I met a wonderful Christian couple named Hal and Deborah McNaughton did God finally give me permission to bring forth this book.

Hal is an astute Christian businessman. His wife, Deborah, is a Spirit-filled homemaker, mother, and businesswoman. She is a public speaker and the head of a powerful marketing firm.

When I met them, I did not know that Deborah was an authority in the area of credit repair. As I spoke with her, I quickly became impressed with her thorough grasp of the credit industry. She knew the law forward and backward, but above all, she had the deep-rooted Christian ethic that would never allow her to advise people to do anything unlawful or unscriptural.

After hearing her speak about proper credit repair, it wasn't long until the Holy Spirit witnessed to me that I should ask her to co-author this book with me. After a season of prayer, she agreed to work with me in this project, for her heart has also been burdened with the need of Christians in this area.

I must say that from the first days of working with her, the peace of God has been with me in this endeavor. He has clearly witnessed to me that the information contained within these pages is the powerful and effective tool for which the children of God have been waiting. It is alive with moral and Christ-centered principles that have been missing from former attempts at this subject.

In this book you will find many little-known facts about your credit and the way it is being reported. I am sure this information will have a rippling effect throughout the entire body of Christ, bringing forth the true nature of God in those who are in Christ Jesus.

Introduction

by Deborah McNaughton

With the introduction of credit reporting bureaus, many have become fearful as they wonder what is actually being reported about them. Questions come to their minds such as, "How are my creditors rating me?" "What will they say if I have had some trouble in the past?" "I am applying for a home loan. What can I do to make sure things are in order?" Many are even saying, "The credit bureau is reporting wrong information about me."

These are legitimate concerns. Having worked with hundreds of people who had inaccurate credit reports, I can see how their fears have almost paralyzed them, keeping them from moving ahead to credit restoration. Credit reporting bureaus can intimidate people. This intimidation then causes fear, sleepless nights, and tormented days. All of this reaction is to something that can be controlled. Second Timothy 1:7 says, "For God hath not given us the spirit of fear; but of power, and of love, and of a sound mind."

The good news is that we have that power and authority, not only through our faith, but also through the provisions of the law. Most people do not realize what their rights are. Congress passed the Fair Credit Reporting Act to protect you with regard to your credit report. Special sections in the law, if used properly, can correct or erase incorrect information from your credit report. The proceeding pages of this book will not only educate you on the importance of having a good report, but will show you steps to correct inaccurate information.

Thousands upon thousands daily face the nightmare of dealing with credit problems and credit ratings. Problems seem to loom from every direction. Many companies have quickly sprung up and then fled with the money of those who were seeking advice on credit repair. These companies prey on the emotional side of people who are dealing with credit problems. **Beware!** They are out there, but you don't have to fall into their traps.

This book will give you information to use when facing credit problems. It can also be useful in repairing your credit. If you feel you need extra help, this book contains information on what to look for when choosing a reputable company.

In 1984 I founded Professional Credit Counselors. Hundreds of clients have come to my office seeking help with their credit reports. I have researched and studied everything available to me on credit, and I have seen the desperation of people seeking relief. Being able to encourage and assist the public in credit restoration has been a blessing to me. I know it was through the leading of the Holy Spirit and determination on my part that I was able to accomplish this endeavor and share the knowledge I have gained.

My office was a teaching center for hundreds of other credit consulting agencies that I helped get started. I have received national recognition through several magazines in the United States for my accomplishments and for my credit knowledge.

Being a child of God, I became frustrated with the lack of knowledge that the body of Christ had pertaining to credit matters. I felt that many people had been duped into unethical practices with unscrupulous companies. It is the responsibility of the Church to keep the body informed of issues that pertain to life. Credit is an important issue. We all have to live with it.

When I met John Avanzini it was surprising to see what God had in store for us both. I had seen John on a telethon two nights prior to our formal meeting. He was talking about his book, *War On Debt,* and I thought to myself, "That book sounds great. I bet I have information on credit repair that he could use." I never imagined I would be meeting with him within two days. My husband, Hal, met John at the telethon and set up a meeting. The meeting was not to discuss credit, but to discuss marketing strategies. Little did we know God had other plans.

As the meeting progressed, the subject of credit came up. With much discussion, John asked me to co-author this book with him. I went to prayer and gave him my answer two weeks later. The Lord has shown me how both John and I can combine our expertise together and share our knowledge of the credit industry with the body of Christ.

It is with much prayer and encouragement that I challenge you not to be afraid to restore your credit. Prayerfully follow the suggestions in this book and you will reap the rewards.

1

The Purpose
Of Christian Credit Repair

There are several very good reasons for writing a book on credit repair for Christians. First, we are told in the Book of First Timothy that God's leaders must have a good report with those who are without (the world).

> **Moreover he must have a good report of them which are without; lest he fall into reproach and the snare of the devil.**
> **1 Timothy 3:7**

Now, that scripture is written to the leadership of the Church. However, the leadership is to be an example to the membership of the Church. So, if God wants the Church leaders to have a good report, one that speaks of fair dealing and honesty on their part, He also wants His Church members to have a good report. The Bible says when our good works are seen of men, they bring glory to our God.

> **Let your light so shine before men, that they may see your good works, and glorify your Father which is in heaven.**
> **Matthew 5:16**

A poor credit report speaks of how your old nature used to lead you. You are no longer to be under that influence.

Those ways are passing away, and all things are becoming new to you, even your way of handling finance. All of this change is coming to pass because Jesus now lives within you. The renewal of your mind has brought about a renewal of your actions. Because of that, a new report must now be made of your business activities — one that will be free of any and all past misrepresentations.

But I Have Good Credit

You may be saying, "I already have good credit. It needs no repair." Please consider this suggestion. Until you see your report, you don't actually know what it says about you. It could contain some major mistakes.

How would you feel if your report showed that an x-rated bookstore and video library said you were a top-paying customer? It could be that you have never even been in such a place, but everyone who read your report would suppose you were a regular customer. Granted, it is not an everyday error, however, as a child of God with a testimony to uphold, it is important that you see your report. You must make sure the information it contains not only is correct, but that it is, in fact, **your** information.

Mixups that show someone else's bad debt could even be on your report. It might be that some vindictive person could maliciously place incorrect information on your report. You will never know for sure what your report says until you see it with your own eyes. So, even if you know your rating should be above reproach, you should get a copy and see for yourself what others are saying.

Some may know their credit rating is bad, but because they are attempting to get out of debt, they figure their report doesn't make any difference anymore. They assume they will never have to borrow again anyway. Dear friend, as long as a bad credit report remains in your file, certain circumstances could cause it to discredit your witness for Christ. There is no reason to take that chance. In most instances, you can get your credit report repaired and make it properly project your new nature in Christ Jesus instead of the old. Once we are saved, we should have, as the Bible says, a good report with those who are without (the world).

A Bad Report Can Block Employment

Another reason to see your report and make every moral effort to correct it is that a negative report can affect your advancement in the business world. Even if you are not going to borrow money, a prospective employer might request a credit history to help him understand your moral and ethical stance in relation to finances.

It is also not uncommon for an employer to ask for a credit report before allowing advancement on the job. A bad credit report could stop your promotion.

If you do contract work, you should be attentive to your credit report. A bad report could cause you to be passed over for a job, even if you are the low bidder. You see, contracts can be awarded or withheld because of your credit rating.

A Bad Credit Report Can Block A Blessing

There is a third reason for every Christian to have his credit report in good order. Hopefully this reason will not affect your need for a good rating. However, at some point in time, it may become necessary for you to borrow money. If the need arises and you have a negative report, you will find it very difficult to do so.

Do not think we are advocating a lifestyle of debt. A review of Dr. Avanzini's other books will reveal that is not the case. However, Christians are at times forced to borrow for legitimate reasons.

For example, suppose your car became so unreliable that it put you in danger of losing your job. That would not be too great a problem if you had saved enough money to pay cash for a new car, but what if you had not? You would have to borrow money for a new car in order to keep your job.

Think of how devastating it would be if some bad information on your credit report kept you from qualifying for that much-needed loan. Your credit information might be outdated. It might not describe your new attitude toward punctuality and responsibility. No matter what, if it were a bad report, it would be a real opportunity for the devil to move against you. The Word of God tells us to give no occasion to the devil.

Neither give place to the devil.
Ephesians 4:27

A bad credit report is a constant opportunity for the devil to discredit your testimony.

Suppose you had the opportunity to take over the ownership of a house valued at $100,000, and all that was required was that you pay the $50,000 mortgage that was still owing. If you did not have $50,000, you would surely want to assume the loan and pay it off as quickly as possible. Wouldn't it be a shame if you had to pass up that $50,000 gift in equity because your marred credit report kept the mortgage company from allowing you to assume the loan? Worst of all, it would be your own fault, for you may have been able to remove those negative remarks from your report with some effort on your part.

You see, even those who refuse to live a lifestyle of debt may need to borrow at some time.

For those of you who desire to have a good credit report with the world, we have written this book for you. It will be of great benefit whether your credit rating is in need of repair or not.

> **Moreover he must have a good report of them which are without; lest he fall into reproach and the snare of the devil.**
> **1 Timothy 3:7**

Section 1
Credit Problems

Establishing good credit in today's society is a necessity. It is impossible to qualify for reasonable time-payment privileges without it. You cannot make major purchases such as a home or a car. Banks will not approve loans. Even owning a credit card will become virtually impossible without good credit.

Proper Use Of Credit Is Necessary

Credit can be either a blessing or a curse. It all depends upon how you handle it. A responsible person will use credit properly and bring forth a good credit report. An inconsistent payment pattern is usually the underlying problem that may cause a bad credit report. Remember, it is up to you how you handle your credit.

Your Credit Report Follows You

If you purchase anything on time payments, a credit rating is inevitable. Seeing to it that your rating reflects good Christian standards is your obligation as a believer. Make no mistake about it. The credit report you establish will stay with you for years. That report will influence your future in many ways. With that in mind, you can see how important it is that you maintain a good payment pattern every time you purchase something on credit.

The Unexpected Can Happen

No matter how diligent you are, things can happen to even the most careful person that can cause severe credit problems. Problems can arise through no fault of your own because of the loss of a job, an illness, an accident, divorce, or any one of a hundred other reasons. When circumstances interfere with your ability to repay, credit reporting agencies can receive bad reports on you.

Credit Problems Are Heavy Problems

Credit problems can be devastating. Once they begin, most people start to feel there is just no hope of improvement. They think things will automatically go from bad to worse. They feel as if a great avalanche of snow is pouring down upon them, and the weight of it quickly becomes more than they can handle. Severe credit problems keep people awake at night, and then these people are not able to think clearly during the day. The relentless pressure of their unpaid bills dominates their minds.

Too many times they either do nothing or react harshly to their creditors. Either way, it simply adds to their problems.

Knowing The Proper Answers
Quickly Brings Relief

Knowing how to deal with out-of-control debt will quickly put your mind at ease. No matter how great the pressure, God designed you to handle any and every problem that comes your way.

I can do all things through Christ which strengtheneth me.
Philippians 4:13

You Are Not Alone

As this book supplies you with the available solutions, you will be well able to overcome each problem, especially since you have the help of the Holy Spirit. Not only will He bring peace to you, He will also help ease the pressure that your inconsistent payment habits have put on your creditors. Try to keep in mind that they also have bills to pay, and they need relief from your problem just as much as you do.

Ignorance Must Go

The purpose of this section of the book is to educate the child of God so that he can properly deal with his credit problems. Believe it or not, the people to whom you owe money are not your worst enemies. Ignorance of what you should do to eliminate your problem is your worst enemy.

Most creditors are eager to assist you when you have credit problems. However, they can't do anything to help you until you begin to communicate with them about it.

You Do Owe The Money

Always keep the following in mind when you deal with credit matters: You have a legal, a moral, and a biblical obligation to pay back every legitimate debt you owe. You have signed your name to binding contracts that promise you will repay. Nowhere in this book will we ever suggest that you not pay back every cent you owe. In fact, it is important that you pay all your bills in full, for you cannot accomplish effective credit repair until then.

2

The Proper Way
To Handle Credit Problems

One of the most frustrating and upsetting situations you can face is not being able to meet your monthly obligations. If that problem ever arises in your life, the first thing you should do is **notify your creditors.** Immediately — the sooner the better — make telephone calls or write letters informing every creditor that you cannot pay.

A Double Benefit

Contacting your lenders at the first sign of trouble is not just for their benefit. It is for your benefit as well, for once you begin receiving late notices and phone calls regarding your accounts, your guard will automatically go up. It won't be long before you begin to feel your creditors are picking on you.

The truth is that when your creditors must contact you about past-due payments, they are not picking on you at all. Just as it is your job to notify them when your payment will be late, it is their job to notify you if they haven't received your payment. That doesn't mean they are angry. It means they are doing their job.

An Informed Creditor
Is A More Pleasant Creditor

If credit problems arise, a creditor you have promptly and properly notified will usually try his best to help you work out a solution. However, if you wait until you have missed several payments, you will probably find that he has become irritated by the extra pressure and expense your lack of communication has caused.

Waiting too long will also cause fear to build in your mind. With that fear will come a doubt that your creditor will agree to work with you for a solution.

It's Never Too Late

Waiting to inform the lender of your inability to pay will always make it more difficult to deal with him. However, just because you have waited doesn't mean it will be impossible to get relief. So even if you are severely behind in your financial obligations, go ahead and contact your lenders as soon as possible.

In Credit Matters, Silence Is Not Golden

Many people who are faced with severe credit problems never contact their creditors. As soon as these lenders see that your accounts are falling behind, they want to hear from you. If they hear nothing, they will assume you just don't care. Without your explanation, they have no way of knowing you are having a legitimate problem. Your silence will make them think you have decided to do something else with the money you owe them.

Different Lenders Respond Differently

As you speak with your lenders about your problems, you will find they will not all be able to help you in the same way. The type of loan or form of credit you have will greatly influence the type of modified arrangements your lender will be able to make with you.

The Solution May Be Smaller Payments

Many times creditors will allow you to make reduced monthly payments. For example, if you have a payment of $25 per month, your lender may agree to accept a payment of $10 per month. The new payment will probably be conditional, based on your agreement to return to the regular $25 payment within a specified period of time. Keep in mind that your creditors will usually be more cooperative if they feel your problem is a temporary one. Any time you can show them you will be able to resume the normal payment at a later date, they are much easier to convince.

It May Be Skipped Payments

Occasionally a lender may allow you to skip some payments by adding them to the end of your loan. For example, if you have a 36-month loan on your car, the creditor might agree to add one or two payments to the end of the loan making it a 37- or 38-month note. That provision would give you two extra months to make up the payments you are allowed to skip. An arrangement of that type can be helpful in getting you through a short-term, cash-flow crisis. Remember, any time you skip a payment, the lender has the right to add the interest cost for the extended period of the loan to the principal of the note.

An Interest-Only Payment
May Meet Your Need

Sometimes a lender will accept an interest-only payment from a person who needs a temporary breather in his finances. If you make this type of arrangement, you will pay only the interest each month. Your balance will not drop. It could be the answer for someone with a temporary financial crisis. However, keep in mind that prolonged interest-only payments are not the friend of the borrower. They do nothing to pay off the amount owed.

You Must Always Get It In Writing

Whenever you make any new payment arrangement with a creditor, always have the new terms written in a letter from the lender to you. Have him state exactly what the new agreement will be. Such a record will prevent any future misunderstandings. When you show him your interest by requesting the agreement in written form, he will tend to look at you as a sincere person with a real problem.

Never Stop Attempting
To Control Credit Damage

When you are making a new payment agreement with your lender, always bring up the question of how it will affect your credit report. Ask him how he will report your new arrangement to the credit reporting agency. Remember, your creditor has shown renewed confidence in you by agreeing to new, temporary arrangements. He does not think you are a deadbeat who will never pay your bills. Go ahead and ask him to continue to give you a good rating on your account. Ask him not to give a bad report as long as you perform properly on the new agreement. If he agrees, praise the Lord, and be sure to get it in writing. If he has already given a negative report, ask him to agree to remove it when you pay the bill in full. Once again, get it in writing when he agrees.

You Must Keep Your New Agreement

Remember, once you have negotiated a new agreement with your creditor, it is important that you carefully live up to it. Keep in mind that when you have had to make a new arrangement, he will tend to watch your faithfulness in repaying more carefully than before. Be sure you do exactly as you said you would do. Don't even be one day late with your payments.

How To Negotiate Properly
With A Collection Agency

If you have allowed a bill to become so delinquent that it has been turned over to a collection agency, you have come to this book none too soon. While your situation is grave, it is still not impossible to repair. First of all, God will help you if you are of a mind to do the right thing. Also, you can do several things to remedy the problem.

Read It All Before You React

The next suggestion may seem as if it would be dishonest or wrong, but let us assure you it is not. You must understand that when a collection agency contacts you, your lender has come to his last resort. He has all but decided you will never pay your bill. His only hope now is to collect a small portion of what you owe.

Many times when a collection agency has your account, the lender has sold your bill to them for only a small percentage of what you owe. The agency may have bought your bill of $1,000 for as little as $200. When you make arrangements to pay the bill, begin by offering the collection agency one-third or less of the original amount in exchange for a total cancellation of the debt. Surprising as it may seem, many times they will agree. If you have any problem with the ethics of this compromise, you can go back and pay any discounts you receive when you are debt free. We know of no creditor who would not gladly accept the balance you owed before making your special arrangements.

Remember, the collection agency has probably bought your account from the creditor for a large discount. So whatever they receive from you above the amount they paid will be profit to them. Most collection agencies go by the rule that receiving something is better than receiving nothing.

Negotiate For Credit Repair

When you work out an arrangement with a collection agency, make every effort to convince them to remove any negative comments that they or the original creditor might have put in your credit report. Press them to do this, even if you must pay just a little more toward the debt payoff than you agreed to in order to convince them. When they agree, **be sure to get it in writing before you make the payment.**

Prayer Changes Things

Be flexible, for there are no hard and fast rules that apply to every collection agency. All creditors and collection agencies have their own ways of handling their accounts. However, there is a way to prepare for the best results with any lender. Bathe your situation in prayer before you begin to take action. The Holy Spirit will go before you and soften hearts. Don't let collectors intimidate you. Remember, it is their job to try to collect a bill that your lender has determined to be uncollectible.

Continue to speak courteously and kindly, and they will continue to work with you.

A soft answer turneth away wrath....
Proverbs 15:1

Always Have A Plan In Mind

When you first approach a collection agency to make a new agreement, have a specific plan of repayment outlined. Before trying to settle your accounts, make out a workable budget. Be sure it is not an impossible one, but one you will be able to live with. Once you reach an agreement to pay off a bill to a collection agency, be sure you make the payments exactly as you have agreed.

Professional Help Is Available

After our explanation, if all these instructions still sound too confusing for you to do by yourself, qualified, professional help is available. We suggest that you check with your church first, for they may have a financial counseling service to help you. If not, make an appointment with your local Consumer Credit Counseling Service. It is a non-profit organization specifically established to help people with credit problems. You can find the CCCS nearest you in the white pages of your telephone directory, or in Section 5 of this book.

Total Honesty Is A Must

If you choose to turn to a credit counselor, always be totally honest. Be sure to disclose all debts you owe. You must also carefully and faithfully fulfill whatever plan he helps you set up with your lenders. Keep in mind that just because you have gone to a professional for help does not mean the lenders have to do whatever the counselor says. Your counselor will still have to convince them that you are sincere in your new plan to repay. It will still be up to you to put forth your best effort to pay all bills in full as soon as possible.

The Sample Letters

On the next few pages you will find some sample letters. They are exactly what we call them—samples. Do not just duplicate them and send them out. You should retype or clearly handwrite them. If you will notice, they are all very specific. Your situation may be totally different from any one of them. However, with these three letters as models, you should be able to write a letter that fits your circumstances.

If you have any doubt about how your letter sounds, read it to someone you trust and get his opinion and suggestions. Carefully pray over these letters before you mail them.

When writing to your lenders, always send your letters by certified mail and request a return receipt. Attach the receipt to a photocopy of your letter and keep it for your files.

Sample Letter to Creditor
(Send certified mail and request a return receipt.)

Date

XYZ Company
12221 Main St.
Anytown, AB 11288

Re: Account 122222

To Whom It May Concern:

In regard to my account with your store, I have fallen behind with my payments and would like to work out an adjusted repayment plan with your company.

I recently was laid off my job, and I am actively looking for new employment. I am able to pay $10 per month until I start working again. I am enclosing a check for $10 to apply toward my account. Please accept this payment and my proposal for future payments until I am once again able to fulfill the original terms of my contract.

I await your reply.

Sincerely,

John Doe

P.S. Please make this letter a part of my file.

Sample Letter To Creditor
(Send certified mail and request a return receipt.)

Date

ABC Company
11111 Adams
Anywhere, AB 22222

Re: Account 221111

Dear Credit Department:

I am writing to inform you of some problems I am having at the present time. My son has been very ill, and I have numerous hospital bills to pay. I have fallen behind in my payments to you and would like to work out a modified repayment plan to your company.

I am enclosing a check for $200 as an interest-only payment on my car. Please apply this to my account. I would like to be able to make this type of payment for the next two months. I feel that I will be able to resume my regular payment schedule at that time.

I await your reply.

Sincerely,

John Doe

P.S. Please make this letter a part of my file.

Sample Letter to Creditor
(Send certified mail and request a return receipt.)

Date

MMM Company
11111 Taft
Anywhere, AB 22111

Re: Account 12223

Dear Credit Department:

My wife and I have recently divorced. I have fallen behind in my car payment. I have a 36-month contract with you. I have only 12 more months to pay on this loan and would appreciate it if you could defer my payment for this month and add it onto the last month, making my contract with you 37 months.

I await your reply.

Sincerely,

John Doe

P.S. Please make this letter a part of my file.

3

Consumer Credit
Counseling Services

The Consumer Credit Counseling Services, CCCS, are affiliated with the National Foundation for Consumer Credit, a non-profit organization. They provide a service to the community by offering confidential and professional financial counseling to those in need.

Whenever the stress of credit problems causes a consumer to feel there is nowhere to turn, CCCS is there to help. If, for any reason, CCCS cannot help you, one of their counselors will recommend other available remedies.

Your First Visit

When you make an appointment with CCCS, a counselor will request that you bring certain items with you to your first visit. He will want to see copies of your recent pay stubs, all of your outstanding bills with the account numbers, and copies of any letters you have received from your creditors. If you are married, you should have your spouse present with you at the initial appointment.

The counselor will also ask you to complete a form that details your family's income, assets, basic living expenses, and debts. After reviewing your completed form, he will determine the degree of your problems and recommend a solution. If he feels your problems are simple enough for you to handle by yourself, he will make some recommendations and outline a program to fit your individual need. If your problems are more complicated than you can handle alone, the counselor will establish a supervised program of repayment for you. He will contact all creditors and advise them of your situation. He will also give them a brief outline of your financial circumstances.

Fixed Monthly Payments

After your creditors accept your new payment plan, you will begin to make fixed payments each month to a personal trust fund set up at the CCCS office. Upon receipt of your payment, all the listed creditors will receive pro-rated checks. That procedure will continue until you have paid all of your outstanding bills in full. On the average, a debt management program lasts about eighteen months. Some programs will be shorter, and some will be longer.

During the time CCCS is supervising your debt payoff, your counselor will be available to talk over any financial problems or emergencies that may arise.

It Goes On Your Credit Report

At the beginning of your new, pro-rated payoff plan, CCCS will notify all credit reporting bureaus that carry your account of your intention to pay off all your debts. Your report will note that you are submitting to counseling and guidance in overcoming your debt problems.

Upon completion of your payoff program, CCCS will notify the credit reporting bureaus that you have satisfactorily completed the debt-management program. The bureau will then add that information to your credit report. It is a negative entry, but it is not as negative as having not paid.

Act Quickly

If you feel you will need help from CCCS, act as quickly as possible. Many of their offices have waiting lists for appointments.

You will find the CCCS offices listed in the white pages of your telephone directory and in Section 5 of this book.

4

Collection Agencies And Your Rights

When a creditor turns your account over to a collection agency, your credit problems have become severe. From time to time, circumstances may arise that keep you from being able to pay your bills. If that happens, the best solution is to make new arrangements with your creditors so that you can keep your accounts out of the hands of a collection agency.

Collection agencies usually contract with the creditors to collect their uncollectible bills for a high percentage of what is due on the bill. Their compensation can be as much as 80 percent of whatever they are able to collect. By that you can see that once a collection agency has your bill, your creditors have given up hope of ever collecting from you.

Collection Agencies Get Rough

Collection agencies have been known to be ruthless in their attempts to collect a bill. There is a story about an irate customer who came dashing into a doctor's office. He was demanding to see the person who had just harassed his wife about an unpaid bill there. The collector had used obscenities and threats to get payment. Upon finding out that his bill had been turned over to a collection agency, the customer left feeling greatly insulted and abused.

Another situation involving a phone call from a collection agency goes as follows: Mrs. C was home ill and received a phone call from the bill collector. She indicated to him that she was sick, but she would mail her payment in the next few days. The bill collector immediately called back and said the agency's attorney would be in the office that day to review her file. If she would come right down and clear up the matter, the agency would take no legal action. Mrs. C became frantic. Leaving her sickbed, she rushed to the collection agency to pay the bill.

We could tell horror story upon horror story of the harassment that unscrupulous collection agencies have used against people who have fallen into their hands. Until recently, a consumer could do very little against their ruthless tactics.

The Law Now Protects You

A federal law came into existence in September, 1977, called the "Fair Debt Collection Practices Act." That law protects the consumer from unethical bill collectors. The Federal Trade Commission has the power to enforce it. To receive a copy of the law, write the FTC. We have listed the addresses of their regional offices in Section 5 of this book.

For your information, we have included a summary of the law:

The creation of the Fair Debt Collection Practices Act came about because of "evidence of abusive, deceptive, and unfair debt collection practices that have contributed to the number of personal bankruptcies, to marital instability, to the loss of jobs, and to the invasion of individual privacy."

A collection agent who communicates with any person other than the consumer to gain information on the consumer's location, must identify himself and state that he is confirming or correcting location information concerning the consumer. He must identify his employer only if expressly requested to do so.

The bill collector cannot indicate that the consumer owes any debt. The bill collector cannot communicate with post cards, or use any language or symbol on any envelope he mails indicating that he represents a collection agency, or that the consumer owes any debt. For example, "Bill Owed! Call Immediately!"

A bill collector is allowed to communicate with a consumer at his home only between 8:00 a.m. and 9:00 p.m. unless the consumer tells him differently. If the bill collector calls the consumer at work and the consumer tells him that his employer does not allow personal calls at work, the collector may not call him at work again.

If the consumer has hired an attorney to handle the bill and has given the bill collector the attorney's name and address, the collector may not contact the consumer unless the attorney fails to respond to the collection agency within a reasonable time period.

Without the consent of the consumer, a collection agency may not communicate with any other individual about any past-due bill other than a consumer reporting agency, the consumer himself, or his attorney.

A consumer can notify a collection agency in writing that he refuses to pay the bill or that he wishes the collection agency to stop any further communication with him. Upon receipt of that letter, the collection agency must stop any further communication except to notify the consumer of any final action they will be taking.

Any time the consumer sends a letter to the collection agency, he should send it certified mail with a return receipt to show the date it was received.

The collection agency at any time may file a claim against a consumer in a court of law to try to collect the debt owed.

If the debt is valid, the best thing to do is set up a payment plan and pay it off as soon as possible.

What A Collection Agency Cannot Do

A collection agency cannot "harass, oppress, or abuse any person in connection with the collection of a debt." The specific types of harassment are:

1. Use or threaten to use violence or other criminal means to harm the consumer's reputation or property.
2. Use obscene or profane language to abuse the consumer.
3. Publish a list of consumers who refuse to pay their bills.
4. Cause the telephone to ring with the intention of annoying, abusing, or harassing any person at the called number.

5. Make telephone calls without disclosing the caller's identity.

False Or Misleading Representations

A collection agent cannot imply to a consumer that he is representing an attorney or a law office.

The representation or implication that the non-payment of any debt will result in arrest, garnishment, attachment, etc., is unlawful, providing the collection agency does not intend to take legal action. Any threat to take action that the agency cannot legally take or does not intend to take is a violation of the consumer's rights.

Payment And Finance Charges

The collection agency cannot add on any finance charges or service fees in collecting a debt unless the consumer authorizes and signs a note agreeing to the extra charge in the document creating the debt. For example, if the bill owed is $75, the bill collector can collect only $75. He cannot add on anything extra, such as a service charge.

If a consumer issues a check post-dated by more than five days, the collection agency must issue a letter stating their intention to deposit the check. The consumer must receive that letter at least three days before the agency actually deposits the check.

Your Right To Verify The Debt

The federal law gives you the right to verify any debt you do not feel is valid. The collection agency, when notifying the consumer in writing of a debt owed, must provide "the amount of the debt, the name of the creditor to whom the bill is owed, and a statement that unless the consumer, within thirty days after receipt of the notice, disputes the validity of the debt, or any portion of the debt, it will be assumed to be valid by the debt collector." That means if the consumer does not dispute the written request, he has no other recourse. No response indicates he owes the bill. However, if the consumer notifies the collection agency within thirty days that he is disputing the bill, the agency must provide to the consumer a verification of the debt and any documentation indicating he owes the debt. Prior to verification of the debt from the collection agency, the agency may take no further collection procedures.

Best Method

By far the best solution in dealing with collection agencies is to pay the bill off as quickly as possible. Congress intended the consumer laws to provide you a chance to work out your problems without harassment.

If you owe the bill, try to pay it directly to the creditor rather than the collection agency. If the creditor accepts the payment, tell the collection agency you have paid the bill. Make sure the agency removes any negative comment they reported on your credit report. If the creditor will not accept the payment, pay the bill to the collection agency as soon as possible.

The law, as indicated, applies to collection agencies. Some creditors have their own collection departments or lawyers where the federal rules do not apply.

If you feel a collection agency is unjustly harassing you, seek the advice of an attorney.

Summary

1. If a collection agent calls, immediately tell the caller that you know your rights, and you wish to know the name, address, and phone number of the agency he represents. Also be sure to get the caller's name. Be sure to write all that information down and keep a record of all conversations and correspondence you have with the agency.

Always remain calm and polite during your conversations. Try your best to resolve the problem and make arrangements to repay in a way you can faithfully execute.

2. If you reach no solution after you feel you have said all you can say, and you do not wish any further communication with the collection agency, write a letter. In the letter, indicate that you do not wish any further discussion or communication with the agency. Send your letter certified mail with return receipt requested. Be sure to keep a copy for your file.

Keep in mind that when you ask them to stop contacting you, the collection agency will probably make one final response indicating what they propose to do and a possible court date. These matters do not always end up in court. Sometimes they will simply write you off as a bad debt.

3. If you have any questions about the bill or any dispute with the creditor, you must write to the collection agency within thirty days of its first contact with you. In your letter, clearly outline your question or dispute. Be sure to keep a copy, and send the original certified mail with a return receipt requested.

The collection agency must then go back to the creditor to verify your bill. During that time, the agency cannot legally try to collect the bill.

4. If you have a major complaint regarding the collection agency and feel they have violated your rights, you have the right to file a complaint with the Federal Trade Commission and the attorney general of your state.

5

Bankruptcy

What about bankruptcy? Is it the right choice for you?

Too often people who are under severe financial pressure mistakenly file for bankruptcy thinking it is an easy way out of their problems. They do not realize the long-term consequences they will face.

Financial problems have a way of tormenting a person day and night. They can cause such mental distress that a person may decide to file a bankruptcy too quickly. If you will take the time to consider what is written in this chapter carefully, it is possible that bankruptcy will not be necessary in your case.

Different Types Of Bankruptcy

We will be discussing two types of bankruptcy in this chapter. They are Chapter 7 and Chapter 13. A Chapter 7 bankruptcy can be filed only once every seven years. A Chapter 13 can be filed at any time, and it is not necessary to wait any specified time between filings. However, before considering either of these, the advice of competent counsel is recommended. Also keep in mind that total honesty in declaring all debts is important to keep from jeopardizing the entire process.

Chapter 7 Bankruptcy

A Chapter 7 bankruptcy is also known as a straight bankruptcy. In a Chapter 7, almost no one is paid. Most people choose this form of bankruptcy, for it has the greatest impact. It immediately cancels almost all debts. That means the person will never have to repay them.

Chapter 7 bankruptcy is designed for those who realistically cannot ever repay a significant portion of their debts. It sounds like a good idea for those who are burdened down with big, unmanageable debt. However, the repercussions continue for a very long time. Chapter 7 should never be taken unless there is no possible way to do otherwise.

When you file for a Chapter 7, you must complete some lengthy forms. On them you will list all of your debts and all your property. The day you return your forms you must pay a filing fee of approximately $60 (the amount may vary). Once you have filed, you may stop paying your bills.

Your First Appearance

About a month later the court will require you to appear for a meeting with the trustee who has been appointed to take charge of your bankruptcy. One of his responsibilities at that first meeting is to see if you have any non-exempt property. Non-exempt property must be turned over to your creditors to help them salvage as much as they can from your assets.

A couple of months after that first meeting, it will be necessary for you to attend a court hearing. At that time the judge will grant a discharge. That is a formal forgiveness of all your dischargeable debts.

The chance of your getting all your debts canceled is unlikely, for not all debts are dischargeable. Examples of non-dischargeable debts are taxes, alimony, child support, and student loans.

Unsecured Debts

An unsecured debt is one for which a person has never signed a written agreement that pledged a portion of his property for its payment. Examples of unsecured debts are credit cards, charge purchases, personal loans from friends or relatives, etc. Those are all dischargeable debts.

Secured Debts

A secured debt is one in which you have made a written promise that if you do not pay, the creditor can take some particular item of your property—either the item you purchased or something else that you pledged. Items likely to be secured include motor vehicles, expensive jewelry, expensive furniture, etc. Most secured debts are dischargeable in bankruptcy. Depending on your original contract, your creditors could repossess some of those items.

Chapter 13 Bankruptcy

Chapter 13 is known by several different names. It is also called "The Federal Repayment Plan" and "The Wage Earner Plan."

A Chapter 13 bankruptcy does not cancel a person's debts. It only restructures them in such a way that he can pay his creditors over a new payment schedule. It is a court-supervised repayment plan. It is designed for those whose financial problems are not so severe as those who might file a Chapter 7. A person who files a Chapter 13 receives government protection from creditors while avoiding a straight bankruptcy.

A Chapter 13 consists of a payment plan accomplished over a three- to five-year period (no fewer than three and no more than five years). Once it is set in place, one must make those payments faithfully until he has completed the plan.

There Is A Dollar Advantage

Chapter 13 has a monetary advantage over simple debt consolidation in that you will pay no interest or finance charges on most debts. The trustee figures your monthly payments to fit your income, and the new budget allows for necessities that people who are overextended many times overlook.

Harassment Must Stop

Upon filing the forms, all creditor harassment and collection efforts must stop. Chapter 13 also stops any garnishments that might be in effect against your wages. From the time of filing, you make all payments through a court-appointed trustee. His responsibility is to see to it that you meet the terms and conditions of your repayment schedule.

A Court Appearance Is Necessary

Approximately one month after you file the necessary forms, the court requires you to appear for a meeting with the trustee. The trustee will want to go over your designed budget with you. At that time he will make sure your plan will work for you.

On that same day you may have a meeting with the bankruptcy judge. If the judge finds that your plan complies with the law, he will confirm it and put it into immediate operation.

At the end of the three- to five-year period, you will go back to court a second time for a discharge hearing. If you have faithfully kept your agreement, the judge will formally forgive any remaining balance due on the debts covered by your plan.

Remember, some debts such as taxes and family support are non-dischargeable. You will have pay them.

Bankruptcies Are Reported

Most people believe that when they file a bankruptcy, their credit reports will be wiped clean. That opinion is definitely wrong! The bankruptcy will actually appear on the credit report. It will also be recorded with the Hall of Records at the county recorder's office.

No money will go to the creditors included in a Chapter 7 bankruptcy. Those creditors will report that fact to the credit reporting agencies. Their entries will be placed in the negative column of your report. That will further hurt your chances of obtaining new credit.

With a Chapter 13 bankruptcy, your credit report will show as a negative entry that you have filed a repayment plan. It will also show the comments of creditors who are being paid under the plan. Since you are making some payment, it will be up to the individual creditors as to what they choose to report about you.

Make no mistake about it. Your creditors do not want you to file bankruptcy because they will lose control of the collection process. If you let them know you are considering bankruptcy, many times they will be more willing to bargain and negotiate a new payment schedule. In that case, you may be able to avoid bankruptcy altogether.

Your credit report can show a bankruptcy for up to ten years, so think about it. That is a long time to have a shadow following you around.

If you have already filed a bankruptcy, do not despair. Bankruptcies are often reported inaccurately to the credit bureaus. The individual creditors involved may also report their information incorrectly. You can always dispute incorrect information. Such a dispute may mean that the bankruptcy entry, as well as the creditor's entry, will be deleted from the report. Know what your report says.

If You Have No Choice

Federal law governs bankruptcy. If there is no other way, and you decide to take bankruptcy, the necessary forms for filing are available from the bankruptcy court in the county where you reside. To find the nearest bankruptcy court, look for the phone number in your local telephone book under United States Bankruptcy Court. You must file with the district where you have resided for the past ninety-one days.

Several good books on bankruptcy that can help you understand the legal process involved are available in the public library. There are also do-it-yourself bankruptcy books. Even though self-help books are available, it is not advisable to go into such procedures without legal counsel. If you feel you must file bankruptcy, we advise you to contact a reputable attorney who is familiar with this portion of the law. He will be able to supply you with the legal answers you need.

Also remember to consider prayerfully the spiritual and moral aspects of bankruptcy. We advise you to seek spiritual counsel from your pastor before making a decision to file such action.

Section 2
Credit Guidelines

The credit contract is a covenant of trust. It is based on honor. Those who extend credit do so believing that the person to whom they have extended it is honorable and will fulfill his contractual agreement. Acceptance of the responsibility to pay for something purchased on credit is a promise that you will not only pay back what you have borrowed, but you will pay it back in the way you said you would.

The Biblical Reason For Credit

The Bible has much to say about credit and the miracle of debt cancellation. The primary reason for credit is found in the Book of Deuteronomy: God said Israel would be so prosperous that the heathen would be drawn to them for the purpose of borrowing. As the lost nations of the world came to borrow from them, they would see that it was the great God, Jehovah, who blessed Israel.

You see, borrowing was instituted as a tool to draw the heathen to us so that we might witness the goodness of God to them. In Deuteronomy 28:12, Moses told the children of Israel that if they obeyed God, they would lend and not borrow.

The Lord shall open unto thee his good treasure, the heaven to give the rain unto thy land in his season, and to bless all the work of thine hand: and thou shalt lend unto many nations, and thou shalt not borrow.
Deuteronomy 28:12

Two Natural Reasons For Credit

Today, businesses extend credit for two basic reasons. The first reason is for the merchants to be able to expand their customer base. Any time a business eliminates the need for full cash payment, more people are able to buy.

The second reason businesses issue credit is to make money. Credit purchasing is not just a convenience. It is a business. Stores, banks, and finance companies that extend credit to the general public do so to make a profit from the interest they charge.

Basically Two Qualifications Apply

Before they grant credit, a company uses two primary factors to determine your "credit worthiness:" first, your ability to repay. Things taken into consideration include your job, income, length of employment, position, and so on. That is the mechanical qualification.

Secondly, they examine your credit history through your credit report. The credit report shows the lenders the amount you now owe and what your past payment pattern has been. That is the moral qualification.

Figuring Your Income

Your gross income is the amount of money you earn before your company takes out any taxes. Your net income for credit purposes is the amount left after taxes have been withheld.

Credit managers usually estimate your net income to be 80 percent of your gross income. They tend to allow 20 to 25 percent of net income for variable expenses such as food, fuel, and utilities. They prefer not to extend credit if your fixed expenses (rent, debts) exceed 70 percent of your net income. Lenders also prefer not to see more than 90 percent of your net income committed to all expenses.

In addition, your employment should be solidly established for at least six months.

If you fall into those guidelines, the secular community usually looks upon you as being financially sound. However, we recommend that Christians do not commit that large a percentage — 90 percent — of their net income to all expenses.

Trustworthiness First

Credit history is usually more important to the lender than your ability to repay. He considers home and auto loans to reflect your basic financial strength. However, the lender will give special attention to major bank cards, travel and entertainment cards, and major department store cards. The reason is that they usually reflect major purchasing power. The world system considers steady repayment over a long period of time to be the ideal credit condition.

Lenders look upon credit extended to you within the last three years as the most reliable indication of further credit worthiness. They tend to favor lending amounts and terms similar to those a person has repaid previously.

Credit Activity

To have what lenders consider a favorable credit history, it is necessary that you have several open accounts. They need not represent debt. Your accounts can show zero balances and lenders will still rate them as excellent. Staying debt free should always be your first priority.

It is advisable not to charge anything to your credit card that you cannot pay in full at the end of each month. If you must borrow — notice we say, if you **must** — for longer than thirty days, do not use your credit card. Credit card companies have such a low payment requirement and such a high interest cost that most of your minimum monthly payment ends up going toward interest instead of principal. It can take you as long as five years to pay off a purchase of $400 when you make only the minimum payment. That kind of purchasing is poor money management. Shop around for a less expensive loan.

6

Credit Control

The privilege of credit is usually available to consumers who keep their credit buying under control. When you must borrow — again we say, when you **must** — a good rule of thumb is that you spend no more than 10 percent of your net income on installment payments. That amount does not include mortgage payments.

If installment debt is more than 15 percent of your net income, you should cut back in some category of your budget as soon as possible. If you are paying more than 20 percent of your net income to installment payments, serious financial trouble is probably just ahead.

Avoid Overextension

To help you avoid becoming overextended, we have provided work sheets at the end of this chapter. If you faithfully use them, they should help you keep your debt from creeping above the 10 percent level. Remember, most people drift off into credit problems. They do not do so on purpose, so if you notice any increases in your debt, you should deal with them immediately.

Four Don'ts

Don't accept credit you don't need. We recommend that you keep about $2,000 in unused credit in reserve for emergencies.

Don't automatically expand your credit when you receive a raise in pay. Inflated costs and taxes seldom leave enough surplus for increased spending.

Don't carry more than three credit cards. The more cards you have, the greater the urge to overspend. Keep in mind that revolving accounts carry lower interest rates on amounts over $500. Having a $1,000 balance on one card is cheaper than having $500 each on two cards.

Always try to use your lowest interest-rate cards. Be vigilant to pay the full balances at the end of each month. If for some reason it is impossible to pay off a card at the end of the month, always pay more than the minimum payment. That will reduce your balance at a faster rate and will save you interest costs.

Don't charge any item that costs less than $25. A significant portion of consumer debt stems from small purchases that probably would not have been made if the consumer had the cash. Don't give in to temptation. If you can't pay $25 in cash for an item, just don't buy it. That small tip may save you thousands of dollars in the long haul.

Know What Credit Costs

Always figure out how much more an item will cost if you must borrow to buy it. Determining how much interest you will have to pay during the length of the loan will help keep you from borrowing when you don't really need to.

Loans and credit cards will charge an annual percentage rate for the use of their money. To figure the total cost of a loan in dollars, you can multiply the monthly payments by the number of months. Subtract the total amount borrowed from the total monthly payments, and then you will see how much you are paying in interest.

For a credit card, some banks calculate interest on a daily basis. Other banks will calculate interest on a pro-rated basis.

Remember, if you **must** borrow, shop around for the least expensive loan.

Don't Decide On The Showroom Floor

Always take home all the figures, including the interest cost, and make your decision there. Never decide to borrow while you are in the store or in the lender's office. Manage your borrowing and do not borrow indiscriminately, then if you ever need to borrow, you will have credit available to you.

Financial Planning Guide
Personal Budget Work Sheet
Please complete this form every month to determine your use of credit.
Make photocopies for use in future months.

Month_____

Income	Projection	Actual
Salaries		
Wages from Self-Employment		
Dividends		
Interest		
Rental		
Capital Gains		
Other		
Total Income		

Fixed Expenses	Projection	Actual
Food		
Housing		
Utilities		
Transportation		
Maintenance		
Furnishings		
Clothing		
Installment Purchases		
Personal Care		
Savings		
Insurance Premiums		
Medical Care		
Dental Care		
Education		
Property Taxes		
Federal Taxes		
State Taxes		
Local Taxes		
Other		
Total Fixed Expenses		
Total Available		
(Income minus Fixed)		

Variable Expenses	Projection	Actual
Entertainment		
Recreation		
Vacations		
Investments		
Other		
Total Variable Expenses		
Balance for Reserve		
(Total Available minus Variable Expenses)		

Credit Control Work Sheet

Keep in mind that we are not advocating a lifestyle of debt. Credit is to be used only when absolutely necessary.

1. Current Credit Obligations:

Name of Creditor	Amt. Owing	Mo. Pmt.

2. Additional Credit Obligation Added This Month:

Name of Creditor	Amt. Owing	Mo. Pmt.

3. Monthly Grand Total

4. Net Income

5. Maximum Credit Payments
   (10% of Net Income)

6. Current Monthly Total
   (from above)

7. Credit Surplus or Shortage
   (Payments minus Maximum Payments)

8. Surplus or Shortage
   (previous month)

7

Correcting Billing Errors

Not all credit problems are the fault of the consumer. Loss of payment through the mail, delayed posting of payments, and clerical or computer errors are the most common credit problems that creditors may wrongly blame on the consumer.

Common Billing Errors

Following is a list of the most common billing errors that can occur:

1. Something appearing on your bill that you did not buy.

2. A purchase made by someone who was not authorized to use your account.

3. An item not properly identified on your bill.

4. An item charged at an amount different from the actual price.

5. A purchase entered on a date different from the actual purchase date.

6. An item you did not accept when it was delivered.

7. An item not delivered according to the terms of the agreement.

8. An error in arithmetic.

9. Failure to credit a payment you have made on your account.

10. Failure to mail your statement to your current address.

11. An item for which you need additional information.

You Have Legal Rights

The Fair Credit Billing Act shows you the proper way to have a company correct billing mistakes. (You can order a copy of that Act from the Federal Trade Commission.) The Act includes the procedure for refusing to make credit card payments on defective goods and even shows you how to have a company promptly credit your payments.

Three Effective Steps You Can Take

If you think your bill is wrong or you want more information about it, follow these steps:

1. Notify the creditor in writing within sixty days after the date the disputed bill was mailed to you. Be sure to send your objections to the address given for billing inquiries. Always identify yourself by giving your name and account

number. Clearly explain why you think the bill has an error. Be sure to state the amount of the payment or item you are challenging.

2. Pay all parts of the bill you are not questioning. One disputed item does not mean you can hold up payment of all items on the bill. However, while you are waiting for a settlement, you do not have to pay the amount in dispute.

The creditor is required to acknowledge your letter within thirty days. Within no longer than ninety days you should receive satisfaction. The creditor will either correct your account or give you a valid reason for not accepting your complaint.

If the creditor is at fault, you will not have to pay any finance charges on the disputed portion of your bill. (To figure the finance charge you do not owe, multiply the interest rate on your statement times the price of the disputed item.) If your complaint is valid, the creditor must correct your account and will send you an explanation of any amount you may still owe.

If the creditor finds no error, he must send you an explanation of the reasons for his determination and a statement of what you owe. That statement can include finance charges that have accumulated as well as any minimum payments you missed while you were questioning the bill. You then have the normal period of time to make the payment, usually thirty days from the statement date.

3. If you still are not satisfied with the creditor's decision, you should notify him within the time he has allowed for you to pay your bill.

Keep in mind that the Fair Credit Billing Act does not allow the creditor to threaten your credit rating while you are trying to resolve a billing dispute. Occasionally credit reports state that the consumer disputes a bill. However, the creditor cannot add a negative comment to your report because of a properly handled dispute. Neither can the creditor take action to collect the disputed amount until he has properly responded to your complaint.

After he has explained the bill and allowed a reasonable time for you to respond, the creditor may report you as delinquent on the amount in dispute if you have not made the payment. He may then take action to collect.

If you still do not agree that you owe the charges, you must inform the creditor in writing. He must then show on your credit report that you have challenged his decision about your bill. He must also give you the name and address of each person who has received information about your account. When he has settled the matter, the creditor must report the outcome to each of those people.

In addition to challenging your bill, you may also request the creditor to place your side of the story in your credit report. We will discuss that in a later chapter.

Your Address Is Important

Keep addresses current with each of your creditors. If you plan to move, it is your responsibility to let them know beforehand. Be sure to complete a change-of-address form and file it with the post office.

When you move, it is easy to miss a payment if your bill is sent to your old address. That mistake can cause a bad mark on your credit report, so watch for your monthly bills. Be sure you receive all of them. If a bill is missing, immediately notify your creditor and ask him to send it to you as soon as possible.

8

Fair Credit Reporting

Before you go any further, it is important that you know what the law says about credit reporting agencies. For your convenience, we are providing a copy of the Fair Credit Reporting Act as amended by Public L. No. 95-598, November 6, 1978, Title VI – Provisions Relating to Credit Reporting Agencies Amendment of Consumer Credit Protection, Sections 601-622 on the following pages. This is as the law stood on November 6, 1978. We suggest that you get a current copy of the law or consult with your attorney to be sure that no modifications have been made since that date. You may obtain your copy by writing to the Federal Trade Commission.

Where To Find Your Rights

When reviewing the Fair Credit Reporting Act, pay close attention to Title VI, Section 611, Subsections A through D. It outlines your right to have accurate and complete information listed in your credit files.

Be sure to read through the entire law several times. Once you feel comfortable with the information you have read, you should be ready to review your credit report to see what you need to do.

THE FAIR CREDIT REPORTING ACT
As amended by Public L. No. 95-598, November 6, 1978

TITLE VI – PROVISIONS RELATING TO CREDIT REPORTING AGENCIES

AMENDMENT OF CONSUMER CREDIT PROTECTION ACT

SEC. 601. The Consumer Credit Protection Act is amended by adding at the end thereof the following new title:

"TITLE VI – CONSUMER CREDIT REPORTING

"618. Jurisdiction of courts: limitation of actions.
"619. Obtaining information under false pretenses.
"620. Unauthorized disclosures by officers or employees.
"621. Administrative enforcement.
"622. Relation to State laws.

"§Short title

"This title may be cited as the Fair Credit Reporting Act.

"§602. Findings and purpose

"(a) The Congress makes the following findings:

"(1) The banking system is dependent upon fair and accurate credit reporting. Inaccurate credit reports directly impair the efficiency of the banking system, and unfair credit reporting methods undermine the public confidence which is essential to the continued functioning of the banking system.

"(2) An elaborate mechanism has been developed for investigating and evaluating the credit worthiness, credit standing, credit capacity, character, and general reputation of consumers.

"(3) Consumer reporting agencies have assumed a vital role in assembling and evaluating consumer credit and other information on consumers.

"(4) There is a need to insure that consumer reporting agencies exercise their grave responsibilities with fairness, impartiality, and a respect for the consumer's right to privacy.

"(b) It is the purpose of this title to require that consumer reporting agencies adopt reasonable procedures for meeting the needs of commerce for consumer credit, personnel, insurance, and other information in a manner which is fair and equitable to the consumer, with regard to the confidentiality, accuracy, relevancy, and proper utilization of such information in accordance with the requirements of this title.

"§603. Definitions and rules of construction

"(a) Definitions and rules of construction set forth in this section are applicable for the purposes of this title.

"(b) The term 'person' means any individual, partnership, corporation, trust, estate, cooperative, association, government or governmental subdivision or agency, or other entity.

"(c) The term 'consumer' means an individual.

"(d) The term 'consumer report' means any written, oral, or other communication of any information by a consumer reporting agency bearing on a consumer's credit worthiness, credit standing, credit capacity, character, general reputation, personal characteristics, or mode of living which is used or expected to be used or collected in whole or in part for the purpose of serving as a factor in establishing the consumer's eligibility for (1) credit or insurance to be used primarily for personal, family, or household purposes, or (2) employment purposes, or (3) other purposes authorized under section 604. The term does not include (A) any report containing information solely as to transactions or experiences between the consumer and the person making the report: (B) any authorization or approval of a specific extension of credit directly or indirectly by the issuer of a credit card or similar device: or (C) any report in which a person who has been requested by a third party to make a specific extension of credit directly or indirectly to a consumer conveys his decision with respect to such request, if the third party advises the consumer of the name and address of the person to whom the request was made and such person makes the disclosures to the consumer required under section 615.

"(e) The term 'investigative consumer report' means a consumer report or portion thereof in which information on a consumer's character, general reputation, personal characteristics, or mode of living is obtained through personal interviews with neighbors, friends, or associates of the consumer reported on or with others with whom he is acquainted or who may have knowledge concerning any such items of information. However, such information shall not include specific factual information on a consumer's credit record obtained directly from a creditor of the consumer or from a consumer reporting agency when such information was obtained directly from a creditor of the consumer or from the consumer.

"(f) The term 'consumer reporting agency' means any person which for monetary fees, dues, or on a cooperative nonprofit basis, regularly engages in whole or in part in the practice of assembling or evaluating consumer credit information or other information on consumers for the purpose of furnishing consumer reports to third parties, and which uses any means or facility of interstate commerce for the purpose of preparing or furnishing consumer reports.

"(g) The term 'file' when used in connection with information on any consumer, means all of the information on that consumer recorded and retained by a consumer reporting agency regardless of how the information is stored.

"(h) The term 'employment purposes' when used in connection with a consumer report means a report used for the purpose of evaluating a consumer for employment, promotion, reassignment or retention as an employee.

"(i) The term 'medical information' means information or records obtained with the consent of the individual to whom it relates, from licensed physicians or medical practitioners, hospitals, clinics, or other medical or medically related facilities.

"§604. Permissible purposes of reports

"A consumer reporting agency may furnish a consumer report under the following circumstances and no other:

"(1) In response to the order of a court having jurisdiction to issue such an order.

"(2) In accordance with the written instructions of the consumer to whom it relates.

"(3) To a person which it has reason to believe:

"(A) intends to use the information in connection with a credit transaction involving the consumer on whom the information is to be furnished and involving the extension of credit to, or review or collection of an account of, the consumer; or

"(B) intends to use the information for employment purposes; or

"(C) intends to use the information in connection with the underwriting of insurance involving the consumer; or

"(D) intends to use the information in connection with a determination of the consumer's eligibility for a license or other benefit granted by a governmental instrumentality required by law to consider an applicant's financial responsibility or status; or

"(E) otherwise has a legitimate business need for the information in connection with a business transaction involving the consumer.

"§605. Obsolete information

"(a) Except as authorized under subsection (b), no consumer reporting agency may make any consumer report containing any of the following items of information:

"(1) Cases under title 11 of the United States Code or under the Bankruptcy Act that, from the date of entry of the order for relief or the date of adjudication, as the case may be, antedate the report by more than 10 years.

"(2) Suits and judgments which, from date of entry, antedate the report by more than seven years or until the governing statute of limitations has expired, whichever is the longer period.

"(3) Paid tax liens which, from date of payment, antedate the report by more than seven years.

"(4) Accounts placed for collection or charged to profit and loss which antedate the report by more than seven years.

"(5) Records of arrest, indictment, or conviction of crime which, from date of disposition, release, or parole, antedate the report by more than seven years.

"(6) Any other adverse item of information which antedates the report by more than seven years.

"(b) The provisions of subsection (a) are not applicable in the case of any consumer credit report to be used in connection with —

"(1) a credit transaction involving, or which may reasonably be expected to involve, a principal amount of $50,000 or more;

"(2) the underwriting of life insurance involving, or which may reasonably be expected to involve, a face amount of $50,000 or more; or

"(3) the employment of any individual at an annual salary which equals, or which may reasonably be expected to equal $20,000, or more.

"**§606. Disclosure of investigative consumer reports**

"(a) A person may not procure or cause to be prepared an investigative consumer report on any consumer unless —

"(1) it is clearly and accurately disclosed to the consumer that an investigative consumer report including information as to his character, general reputation, personal characteristics, and mode of living, whichever are applicable, may be made, and such disclosure (A) is made in a writing mailed, or otherwise delivered, to the consumer, not later than three days after the date on which the report was first requested, and (B) includes a statement informing the consumer of his right to request the additional disclosures provided for under subsection (b) of this section; or

"(2) the report is to be used for employment purposes for which the consumer has not specifically applied.

"(b) Any person who procures or causes to be prepared an investigative consumer report on any consumer shall, upon written request made by the consumer within a reasonable period of time after receipt by him of the disclosure required by subsection (a) (1), shall* make a complete and accurate disclosure of the nature and scope of the investigation requested. This disclosure shall be made in a writing mailed, or otherwise delivered, to the consumer not later than five days after the date on which the request for such disclosure was received from the consumer or such report was first requested, whichever is the later.

"(c) No person may be held liable for any violation of subsection (a) or (b) of this section if he shows by a preponderance of the evidence that at the time of the

---

* *So in original. Probably should be omitted.*

violation he maintained reasonable procedures to assure compliance with subsection (a) or (b).

"§607. Compliance procedures

"(a) Every consumer reporting agency shall maintain reasonable procedures designed to avoid violations of section 605 and to limit the furnishing of consumer reports to the purposes listed under section 604. These procedures shall require that prospective users of the information identify themselves, certify the purposes for which the information is sought, and certify that the information will be used for no other purpose. Every consumer reporting agency shall make a reasonable effort to verify the identity of a new prospective user and the uses certified by such prospective user prior to furnishing such user a consumer report. No consumer reporting agency may furnish a consumer report to any person if it has reasonable grounds for believing that the consumer report will not be used for a purpose listed in section 604.

"(b) Whenever a consumer reporting agency prepares a consumer report it shall follow reasonable procedures to assure maximum possible accuracy of the information concerning the individual about whom the report relates.

"§608. Disclosures to governmental agencies

"Notwithstanding the provisions of section 604, a consumer reporting agency may furnish identifying information respecting any consumer, limited to his name, address, former addresses, places of employment, or former places of employment, to a governmental agency.

"§609. Disclosures to consumers

"(a) Every consumer reporting agency shall, upon request and proper identification of any consumer, clearly and accurately disclose to the consumer:

"(1) The nature and substance of all information (except medical information) in its files on the consumer at the time of the request.

"(2) The sources of the information; except that the sources of information acquired solely for use in preparing an investigative consumer report and actually used for no other purpose need not be disclosed: *Provided,* That in the event an action is brought under this title, such sources shall be available to the plaintiff under appropriate discovery procedures in the court in which the action is brought.

"(3) The recipients of any consumer report on the consumer which it has furnished:

"(A) for employment purposes within the two-year period preceding the request, and

"(B) for any other purpose within the six-month period preceding the request.

"(b) The requirements of subsection (a) respecting the disclosure of sources of information and the recipients of consumer reports do not apply to information received or consumer reports furnished prior to the effective date of this title except to the extent that the matter involved is contained in the files of the consumer reporting agency on that date.

"**§610. Conditions of disclosure to consumers**

"(a) A consumer reporting agency shall make the disclosures required under section 609 during normal business hours and on reasonable notice.

"(b) The disclosures required under section 609 shall be made to the consumer —

"(1) in person if he appears in person and furnishes proper identification; or

"(2) by telephone if he has made a written request, with proper identification, for telephone disclosure and the toll charge, if any, for the telephone call is prepaid by or charged directly to the consumer.

"(c) Any consumer reporting agency shall provide trained personnel to explain to the consumer any information furnished to him pursuant to section 609.

"(d) The consumer shall be permitted to be accompanied by one other person of his choosing, who shall furnish reasonable identification. A consumer reporting agency may require the consumer to furnish a written statement granting permission to the consumer reporting agency to discuss the consumer's file in such person's presence.

"(e) Except as provided in sections 616 and 617, no consumer may bring any action or proceeding in the nature of defamation, invasion of privacy, or negligence with respect to the reporting of information against any consumer reporting agency, any user of information, or any person who furnishes information to a consumer reporting agency, based on information disclosed pursuant to section 609, 610, or 615, except as to false information furnished with malice or willful intent to injure such consumer.

"§611. Procedure in case of disputed accuracy

"(a) If the completeness or accuracy of any item of information contained in his file is disputed by a consumer, and such dispute is directly conveyed to the consumer reporting agency by the consumer, the consumer reporting agency shall within a reasonable period of time reinvestigate and record the current status of that information unless it has reasonable grounds to believe that the dispute by the consumer is frivolous or irrelevant. If after such reinvestigation such information is found to be inaccurate or can no longer be verified, the consumer reporting agency shall promptly delete such information. The presence of contradictory information in the consumer's file does not in and of itself constitute reasonable grounds for believing the dispute is frivolous or irrelevant.

"(b) If the reinvestigation does not resolve the dispute, the consumer may file a brief statement setting forth the nature of the dispute. The consumer reporting agency may limit such statements to not more than one hundred words if it provides the consumer with assistance in writing a clear summary of the dispute.

"(c) Whenever a statement of a dispute is filed, unless there is reasonable grounds to believe that it is frivolous or irrelevant, the consumer reporting agency shall, in any subsequent consumer report containing the information in question, clearly note that it is disputed by the consumer and provide either the consumer's statement or a clear and accurate codification or summary thereof.

"(d) Following any deletion of information which is found to be inaccurate or whose accuracy can no longer be verified or any notation as to disputed information, the consumer reporting agency shall, at the request of the consumer, furnish notification that the item has been deleted or the statement, codification or summary pursuant to subsection (b) or (c) to any person specifically designated by the consumer who has within two years prior thereto received a consumer report for employment purposes, or within six months prior thereto received a consumer report for any other purpose, which contained the deleted or disputed information. The consumer reporting agency shall clearly and conspicuously disclose to the consumer his rights to make such a request. Such disclosure shall be made at or prior to the time the information is deleted or the consumer's statement regarding the disputed information is received.

"§612. Charges for certain disclosures

"A consumer reporting agency shall make all disclosures pursuant to section 609 and furnish all consumer reports pursuant to section 611 (d) without charge to the consumer if, within thirty days after receipt by such consumer of a notification pursuant to section 615 or notification from a debt collection agency affiliated with such consumer reporting agency stating that the consumer's credit rating may be or has been adversely affected, the consumer makes a request under section 609 or 611 (d). Otherwise, the consumer reporting agency may impose a reasonable charge on the consumer for making disclosure to such consumer pursuant to section 609, the charge for which shall be indicated to the consumer prior to making disclosure; and for furnishing notifications, statements, summaries, or codifications to person designated by the consumer pursuant to section 611 (d), the charge for which shall be indicated to the consumer prior to furnishing such information and shall not exceed the charge that the consumer reporting agency would impose on each designated recipient for a consumer report except that no charge may be made for notifying such persons of the deletion of information which is found to be inaccurate or which can no longer be verified.

"§613. Public record information for employment purposes

"A consumer reporting agency which furnishes a consumer report for employment purposes and which for that purpose compiles and reports items of information on consumers which are matters of public record and are likely to have an adverse effect upon a consumer's ability to obtain employment shall—

"(1) at the time such public record information is reported to the user of such consumer report, notify the consumer of the fact that public record information is being reported by the consumer reporting agency, together with the name and address of the person to whom such information is being reported; or

"(2) maintain strict procedures designed to insure that whenever public record information which is likely to have an adverse effect on a consumer's ability to obtain employment is reported it is complete and up to date. For purposes of this paragraph, items of public record relating to arrests, indictments, convictions, suits, tax liens, and outstanding judgments shall be considered up to date if the current public record status of the item at the time of the report is reported.

"§614. Restrictions on investigative consumer reports

"Whenever a consumr reporting agency prepares an investigative consumer report, no adverse information in the consumer report (other than information which is a matter of public record) may be included in a subsequent consumer report unless such adverse information has been verified in the process of making such subsequent consumer report, or the adverse information was received within the three-month period preceding the date the subsequent report is furnished.

"§615. Requirements on users of consumer reports

"(a) Whenever credit or insurance for personal, family, or household purposes, or employment involving a consumer is denied or the charge for such credit or insurance is increased either wholly or partly because of information contained in a consumer report from a consumer reporting agency, the user of the consumer report shall so advise the consumer against whom such adverse action has been taken and supply the name and address of the consumer reporting agency making the report.

"(b) Whenever credit for personal, family, or household purposes involving a consumer is denied or the charge for such credit is increased either wholly or partly because of information obtained from a person other than a consumer reporting agency bearing upon the consumer's credit worthiness, credit standing, credit capacity, character, general reputation, personal characteristics, or mode of living, the user of such information shall, within a reasonable period of time, upon the consumer's written request for the reasons for such adverse action received within sixty days after learning of such adverse action, disclose the nature of the information to the consumer. The user of such information shall clearly and accurately disclose to the consumer his right to make such written request at the time such adverse action is communicated to the consumer.

"(c) No person shall be held liable for any violation of this section if he shows by a preponderance of the evidence that at the time of the alleged violation he maintained reasonable procedures to assure compliance with the provisions of subsections (a) and (b).

"§616. Civil liability for willful noncompliance

"Any consumer reporting agency or user of information which willfully fails to comply with any requirement imposed under this title with respect to any consumer is liable to that consumer in an amount equal to the sum of—

"(1) any actual damages sustained by the consumer as a result of the failure;

"(2) such amount of punitive damages as the court may allow; and

"(3) in the case of any successful action to enforce any liability under this section, the costs of the action together with reasonable attorney's fees as determined by the court.

"§617. Civil liability for negligent noncompliance

"Any consumer reporting agency or user of information which is negligent in failing to comply with any requirement imposed under this title with respect to any consumer is liable to that consumer in an amount equal to the sum of—

"(1) any actual damages sustained by the consumer as a result of the failure:

"(2) in the case of any successful action to enforce any liability under this section, the costs of the action together with reasonable attorney's fees as determined by the court.

"§618. Jurisdiction of courts; limitation of actions

"An action to enforce any liability created under this title may be brought in any appropriate United States district court without regard to the amount in controversy, or in any other court of competent jurisdiction, within two years from the date on which the liability arises, except that where a defendant has materially and willfully misrepresented any information required under this title to be disclosed to an individual and the information so misrepresented is material to the establishment of the defendant's liability to that individual under this title, the action may be brought at any time within two years after discovery by the individual of the misrepresentation.

"§619. Obtaining information under false pretenses

"Any person who knowingly and willfully obtains information on a consumer from a consumer reporting agency under false pretenses shall be fined not more than $5,000 or imprisoned not more than one year, or both.

"§620. Unauthorized disclosures by officers or employees

"Any officer or employee of a consumer reporting agency who knowingly and willfully provides information concerning an individual from the agency's files to a person not authorized to receive that information shall be fined not more than $5,000 or imprisoned not more than one year, or both.

"§621. Administrative enforcement

"(a) Compliance with the requirements imposed under this title shall be enforced under the Federal Trade Commission Act by the Federal Trade Commission with respect to consumer reporting agencies and all other persons subject thereto, except to the extent that enforcement of the requirements imposed under this title is specifically committed to some other government agency under subsection (b) hereof. For the purpose of the exercise by the Federal Trade Commission of its functions and powers under the Federal Trade Commission Act, a violation of any requirement or prohibition imposed under this title shall constitute an unfair or deceptive act or practice in commerce in violation of section 5 (a) of the Federal Trade Commission Act and shall be subject to enforcement by the Federal Trade Commission under section 5 (b) thereof with respect to any consumer reporting agency or person subject to enforcement by the Federal Trade Commission pursuant to this subsection, irrespective of whether that person is engaged in commerce or meets any other jurisdictional tests in the Federal Trade Commission Act. The Federal Trade Commission shall have such procedural, investigative, and enforcement powers, including the power to issue procedural rules in enforcing compliance with the requirements imposed under this title and to require the filing of reports, the production of documents, and the appearance of witnesses as though the applicable terms and conditions of the Federal Trade Commission Act were part of this title. Any person violating any of the provisions of this title shall be subject to the penalties and entitled to the privileges and immunities provided in the Federal Trade Commission Act as though the applicable terms and provisions thereof were part of this title.

"(b) Compliance with the requirements imposed under this title with respect to consumer reporting agencies and persons who use consumer reports from such agencies shall be enforced under —

"(1) section 8 of the Federal Deposit Insurance Act, in the case of:

"(A) national banks, by the Comptroller of the Currency;

"(B) member banks of the Federal Reserve System (other than national banks), by the Federal Reserve Board; and

"(C) banks insured by the Federal Deposit Insurance Corporation (other than members of the Federal Reserve System), by the Board of Directors of the Federal Deposit Insurance Corporation.

"(2) section 5 (d) of the Home Owners Loan Act of 1933, section 407 of the National Housing Act, and sections 6 (i) and 17 of the Federal Home Loan Bank Act, by the Federal Home Loan Bank Board (acting directly or through the Federal Savings and Loan Insurance Corporation), in the case of any institution subject to any of those provisions;

"(3) the Federal Credit Union Act, by the Administrator of the National Credit Union Administration with respect to any Federal credit union;

"(4) the Acts to regulate commerce, by the Interstate Commerce Commission with respect to any common carrier subject to those Acts;

"(5) the Federal Aviation Act of 1958, by the Civil Aeronautics Board with respect to any air carrier or foreign air carrier subject to that Act; and

"(6) the Packers and Stockyards Act, 1921 (except as provided in section 406 of that Act), by the Secretary of Agriculture with respect to any activities subject to that Act.

"(c) For the purpose of the exercise by any agency referred to in subsection (b) of its powers under any Act referred to in that subsection, a violation of any requirement imposed under this title shall be deemed to be a violation of a requirement imposed under that Act. In addition to its powers under any provision of law specifically referred to in subsection (b), each of the agencies referred to in that subsection may exercise, for the purpose of enforcing compliance with any requirement imposed under this title any other authority conferred on it by law.

"§622. Relation to State laws

"This title does not annul, alter, affect, or exempt any person subject to the provisions of this title from complying with the laws of any State with respect to the collection, distribution, or use of any information on consumers, except to the extent that those laws are inconsistent with any provision of this title, and then only to the extent of the inconsistency."

EFFECTIVE DATE

SEC. 602. Section 504 of the Consumer Credit Protection Act is amended by adding at the end thereof the following new subsection:

"(d) Title VI takes effect upon the expiration of one hundred and eighty days following the date of its enactment."

Approved October 26, 1970.

Section 3

Obtaining and Evaluating Your Credit Records

Once you have thoroughly reviewed the Fair Credit Reporting Act, you are ready to obtain a copy of your credit report. Four major credit reporting agencies in the United States compete for the right to sell your credit history to lenders. They are TRW, Trans Union, Credit Bureau, Inc. (CBI), and Associated Credit.

The Information In Your File

Credit reporting agencies primarily identify you by two pieces of information: your name and social security number. They also use your current and previous addresses, your spouse's name, and your date of birth.

The credit information the reporting agencies provide includes the merchant names, their subscriber numbers, your account numbers, the date you opened each account, and the date you closed any account. It also includes your highest credit limit, the highest amount of credit you have used, and most importantly, your payment history.

Payment history is coded into numbers or letters. A series of **1's** or **C's** indicates perfect payment.

Several Credit Agencies May List You

Participating creditors subscribe to one or more credit bureaus by paying them a certain amount of money. They then report the credit activities of their customers, including payment patterns, to the bureaus to which they subscribe. That is how your credit information gets into your credit report.

Every area has dominant credit bureau agencies. Of those agencies that operate in your area, some may have more information on you than others. The reason is that some of your creditors may be members of different credit bureaus. It is important that you have copies of all the reports so that you will know everything reported about you.

You Have Given Your Permission

When you sign a contract for a credit card or a loan, the wording in the contract usually authorizes the prospective creditor to report your payment activity to the reporting agency of his choice. In addition, it also gives him permission to receive a copy of your credit history.

No creditor can obtain a report on you unless you have authorized him to do so. If there is any inquiry on your report that you have not authorized, you should immediately dispute it with the credit reporting agency or directly with the creditor involved.

Turned Down For Credit

If a lender has turned you down for credit, you can request a free copy of your credit report within thirty days of the denial. Each time a company denies you credit, the creditor must furnish you a written denial letter indicating which credit bureau or bureaus he used to evaluate your credit worthiness. See the sample denial letter at the end of this chapter.

When you wish to see your credit report, even though no company has turned you down for credit, the credit bureaus will charge a specified amount to send you a copy.

When requesting a copy of your report, include your name, all of your addresses for the past five years, your social security number, and birth date. If there is a fee, include it when you apply. See the sample request letter at the end of this chapter.

It is important to know that both husband and wife must apply for their credit reports separately. Even if you have obtained all of your credit jointly, you will each have separate reports. The reporting bureaus will charge fees for both copies.

Follow The Instructions

When you have received your credit report, there is usually a section printed on the back that will help you understand it. On the TRW report, the most important thing to look for is the column located on the far left side.

It is divided into three sections: pos (positive), non (non-rated), neg (negative).

You should pay close attention to the non-rated and negative columns. First, you need to analyze if the statements are 100 percent accurate. For example, an item listed in the non-rated column could state "pd. was 90 days late, 3/89." You may have been late paying, but maybe not 90 days late. You may have never been late in making a payment, but the report says you have. Note and dispute any and all errors.

The CBI, Trans Union, and Associated Credit reports have the same type of ratings. **R** means "revolving account," and **I** means "installment account." Ratings on the right hand side of Trans Union and Associated Credit may say "I-3." That rating would mean you are three months late on your installment payments. If it said "R-9," that would mean the company placed your revolving account in collection or charged it off. Anything other than **I-1** or **R-1** is a negative comment. You should analyze all negative comments carefully to see if they are inaccurate. If so, you can dispute them and they can be removed.

CBI reports are a bit different. They show the ratings under the column marked "CS."

Codes

Credit bureaus use the following notations to indicate payment history on credit reports.

Bk Adj Plan — Debit included in or completed through a Bankruptcy Chapter 13.

Bk Liq Reo — Debit included in or discharged through Bankruptcy Chapter 7 or 11.

Charge Off — Unpaid balance reported as a loss by the credit grantor. The creditor writes you off.

Clos INAC — Closed inactive account.

CLOS NP AA — Credit line closed/not paying as agreed.

Coll Acct — Account seriously past due/account assigned to attorney, collection agency, or credit grantor's internal collection department.

CR CD Lost — Credit card lost or stolen.

CR Ln Clos — Credit line closed/reason unknown or by consumer request/there may be an unpaid balance remaining.

CR Ln Rnst — Account now available for use and in good standing. Was a closed account.

Curr Acct — Either an open or closed account in good standing.

Cur was Col — Current account was a collection account.

Cur was Dl — Current account was past due.

Cur was For — Current account. Foreclosure was started.

Cur was 30-2 or 3,4,5 + 6 — Current account was 30 days past due 2, 3, 4, 5, or 6 times.

Cur was 60, or 90, 120, 150, 180 — Current account was 60, 90, 120, 150, or 180 days late on payment.

Deceased — Consumer is deceased.

Delinq 60 or 90, 120, 150, 180 — Account 60, 90, 120,150, or 180 days late.

Del was 90 — Account was delinquent 90 days/now 30 or 60 days late.

Gov Claim — Claim filed with government for insured portion or balance on an educational loan.

Foreclosure — Credit grantor sold collateral to settle a mortgage that is in default.

Inquiry — A copy of the credit report has been sent to the credit grantor who has just requested it.

Ins Claim — Claim filed for payment of insured portion of balance.

Judgment — Lawsuit that resulted in a judgment against you not paid.

Lien — Taxes owed, Federal, State, or County.

Not Pd AA — Account not being paid as agreed.

Paid Acct — Closed account with a zero balance, not rated by grantor.

Paid Statis — Closed account, paid satisfactorily.

Pd by Dler — Credit grantor paid by company that originally sold the merchandise.

Pd Chg off — Paid account. Was a charge off.

Pd Coll Acc — Paid account. Was a collection account.

Paid not AA — Paid account. Some of the payments were made past the agreed due dates.

Pd Repo — Paid account, was a repossession.

Pd was 30 — Paid account, was past due 30 days.

Pd was 30-2 or 4, 5, +6 — Paid account. Was past due 30 days 2 times, or 3, 4, 5, 6, or more times.

Pd was 60 or 90, 120, 150, 180 — Paid account. Was late 60 or 90, 120, 150, or 180 days.

Redmd Repo — Account was a repossession, now redeemed.

Refinanced — Account was renewed or refinanced.

Repo — Merchandise was taken back by the credit grantor. There may still be an outstanding balance.

SCNL — Credit grantor cannot locate the consumer.

Settled — Account legally paid in full for less than the full balance.

Volun Repo — Voluntary repossession.

30 Day Del — Account past due 30 days.

30 2 or 3, 4, 5, 6 + times — Account past due 30 days 2 or 3, 4, 5, 6, or more times.

30 was 60 — Account was delinquent 60 days. Now 30 days late.

Additional Ratings — Manner Of Payment

In some reports an **I** or **R** will precede these entries.

00 — Too new to rate. Approved but not used or rated.

01 — Pays within 30 days of billing. Pays account as agreed.

02 — Pays in more than 30 days, but not more than 60 days, or not more than one payment due.

03 — Pays in more than 60 days, but not more than 90 days, or not more than two payments due.

04 — Pays in more than 90 days, but not more than 120 days, or not more than three or more payments due.

05 — Pays in 120 days or more.

07 — Making regular payment under wage earner plan or similar arrangement.

08 — Repossession.

8A — Voluntary Repossession.

8R — Legal Repossession.

09 — Bad debt; placed for collection, suit, judgment, charge off, bankruptcy: skip.

9B — Collection account.

UR — Unrated.

We have listed the names and addresses of several local credit reporting agencies by state in Section 5. Make a phone call to find out the fees for each report. Check with all four bureaus to be sure that all undesirable comments are in your hands.

Sample Letter
Credit Report Request Forms
Use if you have been denied credit within the past 30 days.

Date

TRW
505 City Parkway West
Orange, Calif. 92667

Dear TRW:

Please send me a copy of my credit report. I have recently been turned down for credit.

Sincerely,

Name
Current Address
Previous Address
Social Security Number
Birth Date

Mail this same type of request to all credit reporting bureaus the creditor mentioned in his denial letter.

Sample Letter
Credit Report Request Without Denial
Use if you have not been denied credit in the past 30 days.

Date

Trans Union Credit
1400 N. Harbor Blvd.
Fullerton, CA 92635

Dear Trans Union:

    Please send me a copy of my credit report. I am enclosing the necessary fee.

Sincerely,

Name
Current Address
Previous Address
Social Security Number
Birth Date

    Be sure to send this type letter to all the dominant credit reporting agencies in your area.

Sample Denial Letter

Dear

    We have reviewed your credit application on behalf of (name of creditor) and are unable to extend credit to you at this time. We based our decision on your credit history of not making payments on time. The consumer reporting agency that provided the information that influenced our decision was:

    ____Associated Credit   ____Credit Bureau, Inc.
    ____TRW   ____Trans Union

    You have a right under the Fair Credit Reporting Act to know the information contained in your credit file. Depending on your state of residence, you may have a right to receive a copy of your credit report at no cost or for a minimal charge. Any questions regarding your file should be directed to the credit bureau indicated above.

Thank you.

New Account Department

    (See reverse side for important information regarding your rights.)

Sample Denial Letter, Reverse Side

Equal Credit Opportunity Act
Notice

The Federal Equal Credit Opportunity Act prohibits creditors from discriminating against credit applicants and/or existing customers on the basis of race, color, religion, national origin, sex, marital status, age (provided that the applicant has the capacity to enter into a binding contract); because all or part of the applicant's income derives from any public assistance program; or because the applicant has in good faith exercised any right under the Consumer Credit Protection Act.

The Federal agency that administers compliance with this law concerning this creditor is the Federal Reserve Bank, 33 Liberty Street, New York, New York 10045.

New York State has enacted section 296 of the Executive Law, which is similar to the Federal Act. The State agency that administers compliance with this law is the State of New York Banking Department, Two World Trade Center, New York, New York 10047.

Section 4

Credit Repair

Before attempting credit repair, we strongly suggest that you pay all your outstanding bills in full. Also, people have found that they usually accomplish the best results if they wait at least one year after those bills have been paid.

If you wish to try credit repair sooner than one year after the final payoff of your bills, you may surely do so. However, we have found that when people do that, the results are usually not so satisfactory. When a credit problem is less than a year old, the creditor can too easily activate your records. A creditor who has just had a bad experience with you is more likely to respond negatively to your challenge of the remarks he has placed on your report. The longer you wait before beginning your credit repair, the less likely the creditor is to respond, which is to your advantage.

Remember that every case is somewhat different, but the actual procedures The Fair Credit Reporting Act outlines are the same. You need to concern yourself only with what your credit report actually states about you and what you can do to have the bureau remove the inaccurate information.

You Are Not The Only One

Thousands of individuals have had to use these procedures in correcting their credit reports. Many of them have had such bad reports that it seemed they would never be able to repair them. Some of those folks could not obtain even the simplest credit. However, after they began to implement their rights under The Fair Credit Reporting Act, they began to receive positive results in cleaning up their reports and re-establishing their good credit.

Those who diligently apply their rights can see as much as 60 to 100 percent improvement. There are no guarantees as to what any individual can accomplish, but we believe you will be surprised at the results you can achieve. Please remember that **persistence** is the key word in making credit repair a success.

Let's now attempt to improve your credit, as well as your Christian testimony, with some credit restoration strategies.

9

Improving
Your Credit Report

It should take about two weeks from the time you request your credit report for the reporting bureau to send it to you. Be sure you apply for your report from every agency operating in your area.

When you receive your report, begin by carefully observing the items that show up as negative information on your form. Carefully refer to the rating definitions that appear on each report. The explanations are usually on the reverse side of the page. You can also review the definitions of the codes given in Section 3.

The Slightest Error Is Important

After carefully reviewing your credit report, make special note of any items you feel have been inaccurately reported. That includes things you feel have not been completely reported. Do not hesitate to note an item as incorrect, even if only a small detail has been omitted. You have a right to contest whatever is written about you and your performance if it is not true. Your right to dispute a negative entry is not a courtesy the credit bureaus are graciously allowing you. It is a part of the law of our land.

No Response Is A Good Response

In Section 611 of the Fair Credit Reporting Act, you saw that a creditor must investigate any dispute on your credit report and remove it if he finds it to be inaccurate. If the creditor does not respond to your objection, the credit bureau **must remove** his negative remark. That means it is to your advantage if he does not bother to respond. You can see why persistence is so important to your successful credit repair.

One Hundred Words In Your Favor

In most cases the credit bureau will give creditors twenty working days to respond to your challenge of the information in your report. If they do not, the bureau **must** remove the negative entry from your report. If the creditors do respond and the bureau does not remove the item, you still have some remedy. The law allows you to place a hundred-word statement on any of the remaining negative items on your report. You can, with those hundred words, explain your side of the story as to why the problem occurred. Your side will then appear on your report.

If At First You Don't Succeed

If you do not feel your hundred-word statement will do justice in explaining the problem, wait four months and begin the entire disputing process over again. Simply make a written challenge to the error again. Repeat that procedure every four months for as long as you feel the creditor reports the information incorrectly.

Do not grow weary. Your persistence will work for you, even if you are dealing with a misinformed or malicious creditor. The reporting agency must dispute the item with the creditor for as long as they feel your claim is relevant and not frivolous.

There Is Help For The Timid

If you feel uncomfortable following the procedure yourself, you may wish to contact a credit consulting agency for help. However, most people are able to accomplish credit repair themselves. It takes only patience and persistence.

Should you decide to contact a credit consulting agency, be sure to select one that is bonded and registered with the secretary of state. Also check their reputation with your local Better Business Bureau.

Be prepared to pay. Credit consulting agencies charge a fee for their services. However, once you have engaged their services, they are responsible to organize your credit repair effort and keep up with the necessary follow-up.

10

Step-By-Step Approach

Step One

Copy the appropriate form to request a current copy of your credit report from each of the credit reporting bureaus in your area. See the sample forms in Section 3.

If you do not know who the major agencies in your area are, call your bank or a mortgage company and ask. As we have mentioned before, the four major agencies are TRW, Trans Union, CBI, and Associated Credit.

If a business has turned you down for a loan within the past thirty days, the credit reporting agency will not charge a fee. If no one has turned you down recently, you must enclose the appropriate fee in the form of a check or money order.

Remember, lenders look at both the husband's and the wife's credit reports when deciding whether or not to extend credit to them. While the majority of good or bad information may show up on the husband's report, the wife's file can also contain good or bad information. That is why you should have a copy of both reports when you attempt credit repair.

Step Two

Approximately two weeks after you have sent the request for your credit reports, you should receive them. A code register will be on the back of each report to help you determine the negative and inaccurate items.

Write a separate letter to each credit reporting agency that shows inaccurate entries on your report. You must dispute each inaccuracy with each bureau that reports that inaccuracy. If one bureau removes an item from its report, it will not automatically be removed from another bureau's report. Each of the four major credit reporting bureaus is individually owned and operated, therefore you must dispute errors with each one separately.

Do not write more than four disputed items on one form or letter. If you need to dispute more than four items, wait thirty days and write another letter with the additional inaccurate information.

Clearly state your name, address, and social security number on all dispute letters you send. Always send them certified mail, return receipt requested. (Regular mail is acceptable, but it is not nearly as impressive.)

Keep accurate records. Your file should consist of a copy of every letter you send, signed and dated, with the signed receipt showing the date the credit reporting agency received the letter. It should also include any letters you received from the credit reporting agency in response. See the sample dispute letters at the end of this chapter.

The credit reporting agencies give creditors twenty working days to dispute your claim. Figure on waiting at least thirty days to allow for weekends and holidays. During that time the credit reporting agency will send the creditor a letter asking him to verify the disputed items. If the creditor fails to respond, the agency will remove those entries from your credit report. That is why it is so important to accurately track the dates of all letters you send.

It usually takes sixty to ninety days for you to receive an updated credit report. The agency will send it to you at no charge. You must be patient during that time. We strongly recommend that you do not try to apply for any credit during the time you are disputing the remarks that appear on your report. Once you receive an updated credit report, carefully check to see which items the bureau has removed.

Step 3

If any items remain that you still feel are incorrectly reported, prepare to repeat the process. Wait four months (120 days) after you receive the updated report. Then begin the procedure again. You can dispute as many times as you wish as long as you wait four months after the date of each updated report.

Step 4

If you are not satisfied with the results, you can add your hundred-word statement to your credit report on any item you are disputing. That statement will be your side of the story. After you submit your statement, ask the reporting agency to send you a new copy of your report with the statement showing. See the sample statement at the end of this chapter. There should be no charge for the updated report.

Step 5

If you are having trouble resolving the problem on your credit report, contact the creditor directly. Occasionally he will assist you in removing the negative item as long as you have paid the bill.

Sample Reasons To Dispute A Comment

1. I do not recall having this account. Please verify.

2. I do not recall ever being 30, 60, 90 days late on this account. Please verify.

3. I paid this account in full as agreed. It was not a charge off. Please remove this comment.

4. This bankruptcy statement is wrong. Please remove it.

5. I do not remember having this judgment. Please remove this notation.

6. This is not my tax lien.

7. I do not owe on this account.

8. This account was the responsibility of my separated (or divorced) spouse. Please remove my name.

The credit reporting agencies must respond within a reasonable time upon receipt of a disputed item. You are trying to get the credit reporting agency to investigate the inaccurate entry. Hopefully the creditor will not respond, causing the bureau to remove the item automatically.

Don't make up a dispute that is not true. Just look carefully at each entry and determine what is not accurate or correct.

You may use the previously listed sample reasons if they apply. If the samples do not cover your situation, you may write a reason appropriate for you.

Sample Dispute Letter

(If the credit reporting agency has a form for disputing,
use their form. Otherwise, write a personal letter.)

June 20, 1989

Trans Union
1400 N. Harbor Blvd.
Fullerton, CA 92635

Dear Trans Union:

My name is Mary Smith, and I reside at 2222 N. 2nd St., Apt. 2, Orange, CA 99999. My social security number is 222-22-2222. My birth date is 2/2/22.

I received a copy of my credit report and have found some items on it that we need to correct.

My account at YYY store, account #11111111 was not paid 60 days late.

My ZZZ Bank account #3333333 was paid off in full as agreed.

I do not owe this tax lien #888888. Please remove this remark. Thank you.

Sincerely,

Mary Smith

Sample Dispute Letter
(Note the date is 30 days later.)

July 20, 1989

Trans Union
1400 N. Harbor Blvd.
Fullerton, CA 92635

Dear Trans Union:

Some items on my credit report are not accurate. I do not recall ever having this account at Brewer's Collection, account #898888. Please remove this notation.

I paid my account at Nelson's Dept. Store #4441 in full as agreed and should have a positive rating. Please correct this mistake.

I never filed this bankruptcy, 2/13/85, docket #2234, for $100,000.00. Please remove this item.

Thank you.

Sincerely,

Mary Smith
2222 N. 2nd St., Apt. 2
Orange, CA 99999
Social security number 222-22-2222
Birth Date 2/2/22

Sample Hundred-Word Statement

October 20, 1989

Trans Union
1400 N. Harbor Blvd.
Fullerton, CA 92635

Dear Trans Union:

Please add this explanation to my credit profile. Make this a part of my credit report.

MMM dept. store, account #111111. In May, 1989, I was laid off my job due to an injury. I fell behind on my payments. I took four months to get back on the job. My debts became seriously delinquent. I made arrangements with my creditors to repay these debts. I have since paid them all off and have a good credit standing. My job is secure, and I am now trying to rebuild my credit.

Sincerely,

John Smith
1111 1st St.
Downtown, NY 00000
Birth Date 1/1/11
Social security number 111-11-1111

11

Most Frequently Asked Questions

1. Does the Credit Bureau rate my credit?

Answer: No! The law does not allow credit bureaus to rate your credit worthiness. They only report what their subscribers report to them. They cannot approve or disapprove any credit requests.

2. Why is an account that I paid off still on my credit report?

Answer: Any account that you have had with a subscribing member of the credit reporting agency will report your payment history, even after you have paid your account in full.

3. How long does a negative entry stay on my report?

Answer: A negative entry can remain on your credit report for up to seven years. Bankruptcies remain on the report up to ten years. Those entries should automatically come off at the end of the specified time.

4. Why don't all my accounts appear on one credit report?

Answer: Some of your lenders may not be subscribing members of that particular reporting agency.

5. When I look in the phone book, there are more than four credit reporting agencies. How do I know which ones to contact?

Answer: There are four major agencies in the United States. The local agencies in the phone book obtain their information from one or more of those four major bureaus. They put the information on their forms and sell them to local creditors.

Please note that when you repair your report with one of the four major agencies, the smaller agencies affiliated with that particular credit bureau will also remove the negative comments from their reports.

6. How did I become part of a credit bureau's file?

Answer: When you first applied for credit, you signed an authorization for the creditor to report credit information to the reporting agencies. In addition, you also authorized him to run a credit report on you. Once you gave out your name, address, social security number, and birth date, the credit bureau set up a file for you.

7. Is my spouse's file a part of mine?

Answer: No! Each person has his own separate credit report. It is based on the social security number, name, and address. To do proper credit repair, you must request a separate report for each spouse.

8. Does the government have access to my file?

Answer: Yes! If you owe any debt to them, the government can receive a credit report on you.

12

Conclusion

Thousands of individuals have successfully improved their credit reports by following the simple steps we have outlined in this book. We hope this information will also help you build a good report for your future.

Be Concerned About Your Report

Once you have cleaned up your credit report, continue to be concerned about what it has to say about you. Make it a habit to order a copy at least once every six to twelve months. You never know when you may need a good report for emergency borrowing.

Remember, be patient and persistent. With those attitudes, you should go far in repairing your good name.

13

Glossary Of Terms

Annual Percentage Rate (APR) — The percentage rate charged on a yearly basis.

Applicant — Any person who applies to a creditor for credit.

Asset — Property such as cash, real estate, or personal property that one can use to repay a debt.

Attachment — In law, the seizure of property; or the writ or precept commanding such seizure.

Balance — The amount owed on an account.

Bankruptcy — The act of having your estate administered under bankruptcy law for the benefit of your creditors. A trustee handles all debts.

Charge Card — A card used to buy goods and services from the issuing merchant on credit, usually due in thirty days.

Collateral — Property offered to secure a loan or credit. It becomes subject to seizure in the case of default.

Credit — The promise to pay in the future in order to buy or borrow in the present; a sum of money due a person or business.

Credit Bureau — An agency that keeps credit records on individuals.

Credit Card — A card that may be used repeatedly to borrow money or purchase goods and services on credit.

Credit Contract — A written agreement between the creditor and debtor that establishes the terms and conditions of a loan. It becomes the basis for enforcing the agreement.

Credit History — A record of how a person has repaid the money he has borrowed in the past.

Credit Rating — An evaluation by a creditor of a debtor's past credit history based on his payment pattern.

Creditor — An individual or business that makes credit available by loaning money or selling goods and services on credit.

Debit — A charge against an account.

Exempt — To be free from an obligation or liability to which others are subject.

Finance Charge — The dollar amount paid in order to receive credit.

Garnishment — A legal summons or warning concerning the attachment of property to satisfy a debt, or stoppage of a specified sum from wages to satisfy a creditor.

Installment — One or more payments due on a debt.

Joint Account — An account that two or more people can use with all of them assuming the liability to repay it.

Late Payment — A payment made after the due date.

Non-exempt — Not released from an obligation.

Prorate — To divide or distribute according to a specific rate.

Repossession — The act of a creditor in taking back property from the consumer who does not fulfill the terms of his contract.

Retail Credit — Credit merchants offer customers allowing them to buy now and pay later.

Revolving Charge Account — A charge account under which payment is made in monthly installments and includes a carrying charge.

Service Charge — A fee charged for a particular service, often in addition to the interest charge.

Trustee — A person the court appoints to administer the property of a person in bankruptcy.

Section 5

Compilation Of Agencies
And Addresses

For your convenience, we have included the addresses of the regional Federal Trade Commission offices, the locations of Consumer Credit Counseling Services, and the names and locations of Credit Reporting Bureaus. This information is correct to the best of our knowledge.

14

Federal Trade Commission
Regional Offices

1718 Peachtree St. N.W.
Atlanta, GA 30367

150 Causeway St.
Boston, MA 02114

55 East Monroe St.
Chicago, IL 60603

118 St. Clair Ave.
Cleveland, OH 44114

8303 Elmbrook Dr.
Dallas, TX 75247

1405 Curtis St.
Denver, CO 80202

11000 Wilshire Blvd.
Los Angeles, CA 90024

26 Federal Plaza
New York, NY 10278

450 Golden Gate Ave.
San Francisco, CA 94102

915 Second Ave.
Seattle, WA 98174

6th & Pennsylvania Ave. N.W.
Washington, D.C. 20580

15

Locations Of
Consumer Credit Counseling Services

Alabama

Consumer Credit Counseling
of Alabama, Inc.
Suite 617, Executive Bldg.
Montgomery, AL 31604

Arizona

Money Management Counseling
711 North First St.
Phoenix, AZ 85004

Arkansas

Crawford-Sebastian Community
Development Council, Inc.
CCC Division
4831 Armour
Fort Smith, AR 72194

California

Consumer Credit Counselors
of California
(State Administrative Office)
1429 Market Street
San Francisco, CA 94103

Consumer Credit Counselors
of Kern County
1706 Chester Ave., Ste. 320
Bakersfield, CA 93301

Consumer Credit Counselors
of Fresno, Inc.
2135 Fresno St., Rm. 210
Fresno, CA 93721

Consumer Credit Counselors
of Los Angeles
650 S. Spring St., Ste. 1119
Los Angeles, CA 90014

Consumer Credit Counselors
Twin Cities
729 "D" St.
Marysville, CA 95901

Consumer Credit Counselors
of East Bay (Oakland)
1212 Broadway, Ste. 706
Oakland, CA 94612

Consumer Credit Counselors
of the North Valley
P.O. Box 4044
Redding, CA 96099

Consumer Credit Counselors
  of Inland Empire
3679 Arlington Ave., Ste. E
Riverside, CA 92506

Consumer Credit Counselors
  of Sacramento, Inc.
1815 J Street
Sacramento, CA 95814

Consumer Credit Counselors
  of San Diego
861 Sixth Ave., Rm. 403
P.O. Box 2131
San Diego, CA 92109

Consumer Credit Counselors
  of San Francisco and the Peninsula
1429 Market St.
San Francisco, CA 94103

Consumer Credit Counselors
  Marin County
(415) 457-3532

Consumer Credit Counselors
  Sonoma County
(707) 527-9221

Consumer Credit Counselors
  of Santa Clara Valley, Inc.
816 N. First St., Ste. K
P.O. Box 1082
San Jose, CA 95108

Consumer Credit Counselors
  of Orange County, Inc.
1616 E. Fourth St., Ste. 250
Santa Ana, CA 92701-5189

Consumer Credit Counselors
  of Stockton
242 N. Sutter St., Rm. 601
Stockton, CA 95202

Consumer Credit Counselors
  of Ventura County
1818 E. Main St.
P.O. Box 192
Ventura, CA 93002

Colorado

Consumer Credit Counseling
  Service of Greater Denver, Inc.
311 Steele St., #30
Denver, CO 80206

Consumer Credit Counseling
  Service of Greeley, Inc.
1020 Ninth St., Rm. #4B
Greeley, CO 80631

Connecticut

Consumer Credit Counseling
  Service of Connecticut
36 Woodland St.
Hartford, CT 06105

Delaware

Financial Advisory Services
  of Eastern Pennsylvania
(Branch office of F.A.S. of Eastern
Pennsylvania)
Dover, DE

Dover Air Force Base
(Branch of F.A.S. of Eastern
Pennsylvania)
Military personnel only

District of Columbia

Consumer Credit Counseling and
Educational Service of Greater
Washington, Inc.
1012 - 14th St. N.W., Ste. 901
Washington, D.C 20004

Florida

Consumer Credit Counseling
Service of Pinellas County, Inc.
314 S. Missouri Ave., Ste. 301
Metropolitan Bldg.
Clearwater, FL 33516

Consumer Credit Counseling
Service of North Florida, Inc.
225 W. Ashley St.
Jacksonville, FL 32202

Consumer Credit Counseling
Service of South Florida, Inc.
1190 Northeast 125th St.
Shore Bldg., Ste. 11
North Miami, FL 33161

Georgia

Consumer Credit Counseling
Service of Greater Atlanta, Inc.
100 Edgewood Ave. N.E., Ste. 810
Atlanta, GA 30303

Hawaii

Consumer Credit Counseling
Service of Hawaii
1125 N. King St., Ste. 204
Honolulu, HI 96817

Idaho

Consumer Credit Counseling
Service of Idaho, Inc.
P.O. Box 9264
Boise, ID 83707

Illinois

Family Counseling Service
411 W. Galena Blvd.
Aurora, IL 60506

Family Counseling Center
201 E. Grove, Ste. 200
Bloomington, IL 61701

Dove, Inc., CCCS Division
649 W. North St.
Decatur, IL 62522

Family Service Association
of Greater Elgin Area
Financial Counseling Service
164 Division St., Rm. 506
Elgin, IL 60120

Central Illinois Credit Counseling
Service, Inc.
505 First National Bank Bldg.
Peoria, IL 61602

Consumer Credit Counseling
Service of Springfield
1021 S. Fourth St.
Springfield, IL 62703

Family Service of Champaign
County
(Budget Counseling only)
608 W. Green
Urbana, IL 61801

Family Service Association
of DuPage County—Budget
Counseling/Debt Management
402 W. Liberty Dr.
Wheaton, IL 60187

Indiana

Consumer Credit Counseling
Service of Tri-State, Inc.
1020 Southern Securities Bldg.
P.O. Box 883
Evansville, IN 47706

Consumer Credit Counseling
Service, Inc. of Allen County
345 West Wayne St.
P.O. Box 11403
Fort Wayne, IN 46858

Consumer Credit Counseling
Service of Northwest Indiana, Inc.
2504 W. Ridge Rd.
Gary, IN 46408

Consumer Credit Counseling
Service of Central Indiana
615 N. Alabama St.
Indianapolis, IN 46204

Family & Children's Center, Inc.
CCCS Division
1411 Lincoln Way West
Mishawaka, IN 46544

Iowa

Consumer Credit Counseling
Service
A.I.D. Center
406 5th St.
Sioux City, IA 51101

Kansas

Consumer Credit Counseling
Service of Greater Kansas City,
Inc.
(See CCCS of Greater Kansas City,
MO)
Service available in KS & MO

Consumer Credit Counseling
Service of Salina
Credit Bureau Bldg.
125 S. 7th St.
P.O. Box 307
Salina, KS 67401

Kentucky

Accept, Inc.—Agency for Credit
Counseling, Education, &
Preparatory Training, Inc.
Speed Bldg., Rm. 407
333 Guthrie Green
Louisville, KY 40202

Louisiana

Consumer Credit Counseling
  Service of Greater New Orleans,
  Inc.
1539 Jackson Ave., Rm. 201
New Orleans, LA 70130

Maine

Credit Counseling Centers, Inc.
175 Lancaster St., Rm. 214
Portland, ME 04101

Maryland

Consumer Credit Counseling
  Service of Maryland, Inc.
Bradford Federal Bldg., 2nd Floor
Fayette St. & Luzerne Ave.
Baltimore, MD 21224

Massachusetts

Consumer Credit Counseling
  Service of Eastern Massachusetts,
  Inc.
8 Winter St., Ste. 1210
Boston, MA 02108

Pioneer Valley Consumer Credit
  Counseling Service
293 Bridge St., Ste. 221
P.O. Box 171
Springfield, MA 01101

Pioneer Valley CCCS, Inc.
(Hadley)
(413) 788-6106

Pioneer Valley CCCS, Inc.
(Holyoke)
(413) 788-6106

Pioneer Valley CCCS, Inc.
(Southbridge)
(413) 788-6106

Michigan

No service reported.

Minnesota

Family Service of Duluth, Inc.
600 Ordean Bldg.
424 W. Superior St.
Duluth, MN 55802

Consumer Credit Counseling
  Service of Minnesota, Inc.
924 Plymouth Bldg.
Minneapolis, MN 55402

Mississippi

No service reported.

Missouri

Consumer Credit Counseling
  Service of Greater Kansas City
  Inc.
3435 Broadway, Ste. 203
Kansas City, MO 64111

Consumer Credit Counseling Service of Metropolitan St. Louis, Inc.
906 Olive St., Ste. 329
St. Louis, MO 63101

Springfield Area Family Debt Counselors
950 St. Louis St.
Springfield, MO 65806

Montana

Consumer Credit Counseling Service of Cascade County
1125 2nd Ave., North, #2
P.O. Box 2343
Great Falls, MT 59403

Consumer Credit Counseling Service of Western Montana, Inc.
P.O. Box 7521
Missoula, MT 59807

Nebraska

Consumer Credit Counseling Service of Nebraska, Inc.
P.O. Box 31002
Omaha, NE 68131

Nevada

Clark County Community Debt Counseling Service
2700 State St., Ste. 11
Las Vegas, NV 89109

New Hampshire

Family Financial Counseling Service
Administrative Office
8 Union St.
P.O. Box 676
Concord, NH 03301

New England Center For Christian Financial Management
CCCS Division
101 School St.
Salem, NH 03079

New Jersey

Family & Children's Service of Monmouth County
191 Bath Ave.
Long Branch, NJ 07740

Consumer Credit Counseling Service of New Jersey, Inc.
76 Mount Kemble Ave.
Morristown, NJ 07960
P.O. Box 97C
Convent Station, NJ 07961

McGuire Air Force Base
(Branch of F.A.S. of Eastern Penn.)
Military personnel only

New Mexico

Consumer Credit Counseling Service of Albuquerque, Inc.
5318 Menaul, N.E.
Albuquerque, NM 87110

New York

Consumer Credit Counseling
Service of Buffalo, Inc.
43 Court St., Rm. 730
Buffalo, NY 14202

Family Service Association
of Nassau County
129 Jackson St.
Hempstead, NY 11550

Consumer Credit Counseling
Service of Rochester, Inc.
50 Chestnut Plaza, Ste. 410
Rochester, NY 14604

Family Debt Counseling Service
of Syracuse, Inc.
114 S. Warren St.
404 Larned Bldg.
Syracuse, NY 13202

North Carolina

Consumer Credit Counseling
Service of Western North
Carolina, Inc.
331 College St., Rm. 212
P.O. Box 2192
Asheville, NC 28802

Consumer Credit Counseling
Service
301 S. Brevard St.
Charlotte, NC 28202

Consumer Credit Counseling
Service of Fayetteville
118 Gillespie St.
P.O. Box 272
Fayetteville, NC 28302

Family Counseling Service, Inc.,
of Gaston County
318 South St.
Gastonia, NC 28052

Consumer Credit Counseling
Service
1301 N. Elm St.
Greensboro, NC 27401

Consumer Credit Counseling
Service
#17 Highway 64-70 S.E.
Hickory, NC 28601

Consumer Credit Counseling
3803 Computer Dr., Ste. 101A
Raleigh, NC 27609

Consumer Credit Counseling
Service of Rowan County
106 Elmwood Dr.
Salisbury, NC 28144

Consumer Credit Counseling
Service
208 First Union Bank Bldg.
P.O. Box 944
Wilmington, NC 28402

Consumer Credit Counseling
Service of Forsyth County, Inc.
631 First Union National Bank
Bldg.
Winston-Salem, NC 27101

North Dakota

The Village Family Service Center
1721 S. University Dr.
Fargo, ND 58103

Ohio

Consumer Credit Counseling
Service
618 Second St., NW
Canton, OH 44703

Consumer Credit Counseling
Service of Northeastern Ohio
423 Euclid Ave., Rm. 401
Cleveland, OH 44104

Lutheran Social Service
of the Miami Valley, CCCS Dept.
573 Superior Ave.
Dayton, OH 45407

Family Service of Butler County,
CCCS Division
111 Buckeye St.
Hamilton, OH 45011

Consumer Credit Counseling
Service of Portage County
302 N. Depeyster
P.O. Box 3010
Kent, OH 44240

Consumer Credit Counseling
Service of Columbiana County
964 N. Market St.
P.O. Box 213
Lisbon, OH 44432

Consumer Credit Counseling
Program
122 W. Church St.
Newark, OH 43055

Children's & Family Service
Association
CCCS of the Upper Ohio Valley
Steubenville, OH
(614) 283-4763

Consumer Credit Counseling
Program
1704 N. Road, S.E.
Heaton, OH 44484

Children's & Family Service
CCCS Division
535 Marmion Ave.
Youngstown, OH 44502

Oklahoma

Consumer Credit Counseling
Service of Central Oklahoma, Inc.
2519 Northwest 23rd
P.O. Box 75405
Oklahoma City, OK 73147

Credit Counseling Centers
of Oklahoma, Inc.
2140 S. Harvard, Ste. 110
P.O. Box 4450
Tulsa, OK 74104

Oregon

Consumer Credit Counseling
Service of Linn-Benton, Inc.
201 W. First
P.O. Box 1006
Albany, OR 97321

Consumer Credit Counseling
Service of Central Oregon, Inc.
2115 NE 1st St., Ste. A
Bend, OR 97701

Consumer Credit Counseling
Service of Lane County, Inc.
110 East 16th
Eugene, OR 97401

Consumer Credit Counseling
Service of Southern Oregon, Inc.
10 North Central, #4
Medford, OR 97501

Coos-Curry Consumer Credit
Counseling Service
Pony Village
North Bend, OR 97459

Consumer Credit Counseling
Service of Oregon, Inc.
4320 SE Powell Blvd.
P.O. Box 42155
Portland, OR 97242

Consumer Credit Counseling
Service of Roseburg, Inc.
P.O. Box 1011
Roseburg, OR 97470

Consumer Credit Counseling
Service of Mid-Willamette
Valley, Inc.
665 Cottage, N.E.
Salem, OR 97301

Pennsylvania

Consumer Credit Counseling
Service of Lehigh Valley, Inc.
411 Walnut
Allentown, PA 18101

Financial Advisory Services
of Eastern Pennsylvania
Constitution Bldg., Ste. 202
1950 Street Road
Cornwells Heights, PA 19020

Consumer Credit Counseling
Service
155 West 8th St., Ste. 216
Erie, PA 16501

Consumer Credit Counseling
Service of Delaware Valley
1211 Chestnut Ave. Rm. 411
Philadelphia, PA 19107

Consumer Credit Counseling
Service of Western Pennsylvania,
Inc.
Suite 510, The Bank Tower
307 Fourth Ave.
Pittsburgh, PA 15222

Consumer Credit Counseling
  Service of Northeastern
  Pennsylvania
402 Connell Bldg.
North Washington St.
Scranton, PA 18503

Rhode Island

Consumer Credit Counseling
  Division, Rhode Island
  Consumers Council
365 Broadway
Providence, RI 02909

South Carolina

Consumer Credit Counseling
  Service of Greater Charleston,
  S.C.
3005 W. Montague
Charleston, SC 29405

Family Service Center
1800 Main St.
Columbia, SC 29201

Family Counseling Service
300 University Ridge, Ste. 108
P.O. Box 10306
Federal Station
Greenville, SC 29603

South Dakota

Consumer Credit Counseling
  Service of the Black Hills
P.O. Box 14
7th and Kansas City Streets
Rapid City, SD 57701

Tennessee

Family & Children's Services
  of Chattanooga
CCCS Division
317 Oak St., Ste. 316
Chattanooga, TN 37403

Consumer Credit Counseling
  Service of Greater Knoxville, Inc.
705 Broadway, Ste. 200
Knoxville, TN 37917

Credit Counseling Service
  of Memphis-Shelby County
81 Madison, Ste. 1112
Memphis, TN 38103

Consumer Credit Counseling
  Service of Metropolitan Nashville
109 Third Ave., North
Nashville, TN 37201

Texas

Child & Family Service
CCCS Division
419 W. Sixth Street
Austin, TX 78701

Money Management Counseling
  & Services
3210 Reid Dr., Ste. 8-A
Corpus Christi, TX 78404

Consumer Credit Counseling
  Service of Greater Dallas
4447 North Central Expressway
Dallas, TX 75205

Consumer Credit Counseling
Service of Greater Fort Worth
807 Texas St., Ste. 104
Fort Worth, TX 76102

Consumer Credit Counseling
Service of Houston & the Gulf
Coast Area
3215 Fannin St.
Houston, TX 77004

Consumer Credit Counseling
of North Central Texas, Inc.
203-A W. Louisiana St.
McKinney, TX 75069

Utah

Consumer Credit Counseling
Service of Utah, Inc.
220 E., 3900 S., Ste. 1
Salt Lake City, Utah 84107

Vermont

Family Financial Counseling
(603) 224-6593

Virginia

Consumer Credit Counseling &
Educational Service of Northern
Virginia
(Branch of CCCS, Washington,
D.C.)
6911 Richmond Hwy., #240
Alexandria, VA 22306

Consumer Credit Counseling &
Educational Service of Northern
Virginia
(Branch of CCCS, Washington,
D.C.)
3451 Chain Bridge Rd., Ste. 3-A
Fairfax, VA 22030

Peninsula Family Service &
Travelers Aid, Inc.
CCCS Division
1520 Aberdeen Rd.
P.O. Box 7315
Hampton, VA 23666

Consumer Credit Counseling
Service of Tidewater
222 - 19th St. West
Norfolk, VA 23517

Consumer Credit Counseling
Service of Greater Richmond,
Inc.
6 North 6th St., Ste. 301
Richmond, VA 23219

Consumer Credit Counseling
of Roanoke Valley, Inc.
920 S. Jefferson St.
Suite 209, Carlton Terrace Bldg.
Roanoke, VA 24016

Washington

Consumer Credit Counseling
Service of the Tri-Cities
113 W. Kennewick Ave.
P.O. Box 6551
Kennewick, WA 99336

Consumer Credit Counseling
  Service of Seattle
2316 Sixth Ave.
Seattle, WA 98121

Consumer Credit Counseling
  Service of Tacoma-Pierce
11300 Bridgeport Way, SW, Ste. D
Tacoma, WA 98499

Consumer Credit Counseling
  Service of Yakima Valley
412 South 3rd St.
Yakima, WA 98901

West Virginia

Consumer Credit Counseling
  Service of Kanawha Valley
503 Terminal Bldg.
8 Capitol St.
Charleston, WV 25301

Consumer Credit Counseling
  of Family Service, Inc.
1007 Fifth Ave.
Huntington, WV 25701

Consumer Credit Counseling
  Service of the Mid-Ohio Valley,
  Inc.
410 1/2 Market St.
P.O. Box 454
Parkersburg, WV 26101

Children & Family Service
  Association, CCCS of the Upper
  Ohio Valley
11th and Chaplin Streets
Wheeling, WV 26003

Wisconsin

Madison Consumer Credit
  Counseling Service
214 N. Hamilton St.
Madison, WI 53703

Wyoming

Consumer Credit Counseling
  Service of Wyoming, Inc.
145 West 9th
P.O. Box 215
Casper, WY 82601

16

Credit Reporting Bureaus

Associated Credit Offices

Illinois

Associated Credit Services
3025 Salt Creek Ln.
Arlington Heights, IL 60005
(312) 259-6801

Indiana

Credit Bureau of Elkhart
116 S. Second St.
P. O. Box 337
Elkhart, IN 46514
(219) 293-1511

Associated Credit Services
2 W. Washington, Suite 811
Indianapolis, IN 46204
(317) 633-1500

Credit Bureau of Marion
American Bank Bldg.
P. O. Box 658
Marion, IN 46952
(317) 664-8001

Credit Bureau Services
2424 S. Franklin St.
P. O. Box 1040
Michigan City, IN 46360
(219) 872-0547

Credit Bureau
  South Bend-Mishawaka
312 W. Colfax Ave.
P. O. Box 1751
South Bend, IN 46634
(219) 236-5600

Credit Bureau of Terre Haute
1401 Margaret Ave.
P. O. Box 1504
Terre Haute, IN 47802
(812) 235-4570

Iowa

Credit Bureau of Council Bluffs
225 S. Main St.
P. O. Box 186
Council Bluffs, IA 51501
(712) 328-1581

Credit Bureau of Cedar Rapids
200 S.G.A. Bldg.
P. O. Box 4291
Cedar Rapids, IA 52401
(319) 365-0401

Credit Bureau of Des Moines
600 Insurance Exchange Bldg.
5th and Grand Ave.
P. O. Box 1817
Des Moines, IA 50309
(515) 247-8900

Credit Bureau of Waterloo
2014 Byron Ave.
P. O. Box 900
Waterloo, IA 50705
(319) 235-1441

Kansas

Affiliated Credit Bureaus
212 S. Market
Wichita, KS 67202
(316) 263-9161

Louisiana

Credit Bureau of Lake Charles
510 Clarence St.
P. O. Box 945
Lake Charles, LA 70602
(318) 439-9401

Credit Bureau of Opelousas
P. O. Box 535
Opelousas, LA 70570
(318) 948-3622

Credit Bureau Covington/Slidell
P. O. Drawer S
Slidell, LA 70459
(504) 643-1367

Minnesota

Credit Bureau of Duluth
21 E. Superior
Duluth, MN 55802
(218) 722-2861

Associated Credit Services
700 Plymouth Bldg.
Minneapolis, MN 55402
(612) 370-9270

Affiliated Credit Services
316 ½ First Ave., SW
Rochester, MN 55901
(507) 228-0145

Credit Bureau of St. Cloud
1116 St. Germain St.
P. O. Box 99
St. Cloud, MN 56301
(612) 252-4800

Missouri

Credit Bureau of SE Missouri
1636 Independence
Cape Girardeau, MO 63701
(314) 334-6044

Credit Bureau of Columbia
515 Tandy
P. O. Box 973
Columbia, MO 65201
(314) 875-2551

Credit Bureau of Jefferson City
238 E. High St.
P. O. Box 359
Jefferson City, MO 65102
(314) 635-6891

Credit Bureau of Joplin
212 ½ W. Fifth St.
P. O. Box 221
Joplin, MO 64801
(417) 623-5200

Credit Bureau
 of Greater Kansas City
906 Grand Ave., Suite 300
P. O. Box 476
Kansas City, MO 64106
(816) 221-5600

Credit Bureau of Springfield
950 St. Louis Street
P. O. Box 1325
Springfield, MO 65805
(417) 862-3711

Credit Bureau Services
11700 Concord Village Ave.
St. Louis, MO 63128
(314) 849-6800

North Carolina

Credit Bureau of Burlington
507 S. Church St.
Burlington, NC 27215
(919) 229-5362

Credit Bureau of North Carolina
106 Broad St.
P. O. Box 1004
Dunn, NC 28334
(919) 892-7117

Credit Bureau E. North Carolina
301 Henderson Dr.
Jacksonville, NC 28540
(919) 455-4141

Roanoke Rapids Area
 Credit Bureau
P. O. Box 519
Roanoke Rapids, NC 27870
(919) 537-4157

North Dakota

Credit Bureau of Fargo-Moorhead
101 S. 8th St.
P. O. Box 430
Fargo ND 58107
(701) 293-1434

Credit Bureau of Grand Forks
11 S. Fourth St., Suite B-2
P. O. Box 246
Grand Forks, ND 58201
(701) 775-8165

Ohio

Credit Bureau of Akron, Inc.
2641 W. Market St.
Akron, OH 44313
(216) 867-0780

Credit Bureau of Canton, OH
128 Third St. NE
P. O. Box 1033
Canton, OH 44702
(216) 456-5941

Credit Bureau Services
  Southeast Ohio
155 S. Watt St.
Chillicothe, OH 43215
(614) 773-2181

Credit Bureau of Cincinnati
309 Vine St.
P. O. Box 1239
Cincinnati, OH 45202
(513) 651-6200

CBC Credit Services
One Playhouse Square
1375 Euclid Ave., Suite 510
Cleveland, OH 44115
(216) 241-4066

CBC Companies
170 E. Town St.
Columbus, OH 45601
(614) 222-5300

Credit Bureau of Delaware
170 E. Town St.
Columbus, OH 45601
(614) 369-2040

Dayton Credit Services
3 E. Second St., Suite 222
Dayton, OH 45402
(513) 224-1005

Credit Bureau Mansfield-Ashland
390 Marion Ave.
Mansfield, OH 44902
(419) 524-4111

Credit Bureau of Newark
141 W. Main St.
P. O. Box F
Newark, OH 43055
(614) 345-6651

Credit Bureau of Springfield
20 W. Columbia St.
P. O. Box 1968
Springfield, OH 45502
(513) 323-4666

Oklahoma

Associated Credit Services
121 S. Santa Fe
P. O. Box 1207
Norman, OK 73069
(405) 329-8705

Credit Bureau of Tulsa
615 S. Detroit
P. O. Box 3424
Tulsa, OK 74101
(918) 587-1261

South Carolina

Credit Bureau of Myrtle Beach
406A Main
Conway, SC 29526

Credit Bureau of Myrtle Beach
P. O. Box 315
Myrtle Beach, SC 29578
(803) 248-4513

South Dakota

Credit Bureau of Sioux Falls
317 ½ S. Phillips Ave.
P. O. Box 1403
Sioux Falls, SD 57102
(605) 336-0470

Tennessee

Credit Bureau of Cleveland, TN
215 Second St. NW
P. O. Box 1015
Cleveland, TN 37311
(612) 472-5431

Texas

Amarillo Credit Association
912 S. Taylor St.
P. O. Box 470
Amarillo, TX 79184
(806) 374-1611
(806) 374-3758

Merchants and Professional CB
P. O. Box 1623
Austin, TX 78767
(512) 458-6122

Credit Bureau Greater Beaumont
4347 Phelan
P. O. Box 3030
Beaumont, TX 77704
(409) 898-4731

Credit Bureau of Corpus Christi
723 Upper North Broadway
P. O. Box 1269
Corpus Christi, TX 78403
(512) 884-2851

Associated Credit Services
1701 Greenville Ave., Suite 1120
Richardson (Dallas), TX 75081
(214) 231-9525

Associated Credit Services
2100 Travis St.
Houston, TX 77002
(713) 652-3400

Network Headquarters:
Associated Credit Services
National Sales Office
2505 Fannin St.
Houston, TX 77002
(713) 652-3360

Credit Bureau Brazoria County
104B This Way
P. O. Box 1548
Lake Jackson, TX 77566
(713) 331-4411

Retail Merchants Association
902 Avenue J
P. O. Box 2249
Lubbock, TX 79408
(806) 763-2811

Credit Bureau of E. Texas
405 E. Hospital St.
P. O. Box 947
Nacogdoches, TX 75961
(409) 564-7341

Credit Bureau of Odessa
2105 Andrews Hwy.
P. O. Box 4593
Odessa, TX 79760
(915) 332-8782

Credit Bureau S. Central Texas
806 N. Austin
P. O. Box 670
Seguin, TX 78155
(512) 379-1350

Credit Bureau of Victoria
516 N. Main
P. O. Box 1699
Victoria, TX 77901
(512) 573-9161

ACS/Waco Area
3901 W. Waco Dr.
Waco, TX 76710
(817) 754-7277

Virginia

Associated Credit Services
11 Koger Executive Center,
  Suite 100A
Norfolk, VA 23502
(804) 466-1554

Retail Merchants Association
14 Franklin St.
P. O. Drawer 990
Petersburg, VA 23804
(804) 733-4611

West Virginia

Credit Bureau of Charleston
2nd Fl., Terminal Bldg.
P. O. Box 1707
Charleston, WV 25326
(304) 343-6111

Black Diamond Credit Bureau
730 Rear Alderson St.
P. O. Box 1782
Williamson, WV 25661
(304) 235-7574

CBI Locations

Alabama

CBI Credit Bureau
Chamber/Commerce Bldg.
Anniston, AL 36201
(205) 237-5484

CBI Credit Bureau
2119 First Ave. North
Birmingham, AL 35202
(205) 252-7121

California

CBI of San Jose
6389 San Ignacio Ave.
San Jose, CA 95119
(408) 629-3377

CBI of Santa Rosa
P. O. Box 6185
Santa Rosa, CA 95406
(707) 546-0550

Connecticut

CBI of Bridgeport
Golden Hill
Bridgeport, CT 06611
(203) 366-7951

District of Columbia

CBI Credit Bureau
P. O. Box 1617
Washington, D.C. 20013
(301) 891-3100

Florida

CBI Credit Bureau
P. O. Box 680010
Miami, FL 33168
(305) 685-5911

CBI Credit Bureau
P. O. Box 4008
Sarasota, FL 32789
(813) 924-1181

CBI Credit Bureau
P. O. Box 32790
Winter Park, FL 32790
(305) 647-1400

Georgia

CBI Headquarters
P. O. Box 95007
Atlanta, GA 30347
(404) 325-0118

Idaho

CBI Credit Bureau
6100 Emerald
Boise, ID 83704
(208) 376-2122

Maryland

CBI of Maryland
P. O. Box 1617
Washington, D.C. 20013
(301) 891-3000

Mississippi

CBI Credit Bureau
P. O. Box 299
Gulf Port, MS 39502
(601) 863-7171

CBI Regional
P. O. Box 2363
Tupelo, MS 38801
(601) 842-2424

Montana

CBI Credit Bureau
P. O. Box 9
Wahoo, MT 59072
(406) 968-3665

New York

CBI Credit Bureau
Three Corporate Plaza
Albany, NY 12203
(518) 869-6699

CBI Credit Bureau
20 Braodway
Massasspequa, NY 11758
(516) 795-8000

North Carolina

CBI Credit Bureau
P. O. Box 26868
Raleigh, NC 27611
(919) 876-1460

South Carolina

CBI Credit Bureau
223 Stoneridge Dr.
Columbia, SC 29210
(803) 256-2206

Virginia

CBI Credit Bureau
5755 Poplar Hall Dr.
Norfolk, VA 23502
(804) 466-1600

TRW Information Services and Independent Bureau Offices

Alaska

Credit Bureau of Alaska
P. O. Box 4-C
3400 Spenard Rd.
Anchorage, AK 99509
(907) 279-5689

Arizona

Credit Data of Arizona, Inc.
P. O. Box 2070
Phoenix, AZ 85001
(602) 252-6951

Credit Bureau of Safford
608 Main
P. O. Box 426
Safford, AZ 85546
(602) 428-1610

Credit Bureau of Pinetop
Pinecrest Rd. & Hillside Dr.
Box 69
Pinetop, AZ 85935
(602) 336-4137

Credit Data of Arizona, Inc.
5055 E. Broadway, #A-206
Tucson, AZ 85716
(602) 372-7403

California

TRW Information Services
505 City Parkway West
P. O. Box 6230
Orange, CA 92667
(714) 937-2000
(213) 254-6871 (24-Hr. Recording)
(714) 991-5100 (24-Hr. Recording)

TRW Information Services
1300 E. Shaw Avenue, Suite 147
Fresno, CA 93710
(209) 226-5271
(209) 225-1998 (24-Hr. Recording)

TRW Information Services
2423 Camino Del Rio South,
  Suite 103
San Diego, CA 92108
(619) 291-4525
(619) 296-0148 (24-Hr. Recording)

TRW Information Services
One Harbor Drive, Suite 110
Sausalito, CA 94965
(415) 331-1TRW
(415) 571-0111 (24-Hr. Recording)

TRW Information Services
106 Park Center Plaza
San Jose, CA 95113
(408) 293-8556
(408) 293-7750 (24-Hr. Recording)

TRW Information Services
966 Fulton Avenue
Sacramento, CA 95825
(916) 481-9232
(916) 481-3115 (24-Hr. Recording)

Credit Association of Humboldt
P. O. Box 164
1201 Fifth Street
Eureka, CA 95501
(707) 443-3041

Empire Credit Data
166 East Gobbi Street
P. O. Box 1426
Ukiah, CA 95482
(707) 443-3041

Credit Bureau
  of Monterey Peninsula, Inc.
P. O. Box 1631
801 Lighthouse Avenue
Monterey, CA 93940
(408) 375-2211

Credit Data North
748 North Market Street
Redding, CA 96001
(916) 243-5800

Credit Data of Oregon, Inc.
748 North Market St.
Redding, CA 96001
(916) 243-5800

Credit Bureau of Salinas
41 East San Luis St.
Salinas, CA 93902
(408) 424-3916

Credit Bureau Data Service
22789 Foothill Blvd.
Hayward, CA 94543
(415) 582-6568

Credit Bureau of Greater
  Santa Cruz, Inc.
1541-D Pacific Ave.
Santa Cruz, CA 95060
(408) 426-5700

Colorado

TRW Information Services
2260 So. Xanadu Way
Aurora, CO 80014
(303) 695-8999 –
  Administration/Marketing
(303) 695-4786 –
  Consumer Relations

Connecticut

TRW Information Services
211 State St., Room 418
Bridgeport, CT 06604
(203) 335-3164
(203) 579-7857

District of Columbia

TRW Information Services
5565 Sterrett Pl.
Clark Bldg., Suite 527
Columbia, MD 21044
(301) 992-3000 Baltimore
(301) 992-3055 Baltimore (24-Hr.
  Recording)
(301) 953-2360 Washington D.C.
(301) 596-4811 Washington D.C.

Florida

TRW Information Services
1525 N.W. 167th St., Suite 320
Miami, FL 33169
(305) 624-8471
(305) 625-7858 (English & Spanish
  24-Hr. Recording)

Credit Data Services, Inc.
1320 North Semoran
Orlando, FL 32807
(305) 282-6500

Credit Services, Inc.
P. O. Box 1888
Titusville, FL 32780
(305) 267-3811

Credit Data Services, Inc.
5750 North Hoover Blvd., Bldg. B
Tampa, FL 33614
(813) 886-7177

Credit Data Services, Inc.
P. O. Box 969
1961 Dixie Ave.
Vero Beach, FL 32960
(305) 567-4303

Georgia

TRW Information Services
6303 Barfield Rd., N.E., Suite 206
Atlanta, GA 30328
(404) 255-7242

Merchants Credit Bureau
955 Greene St.
Augusta, GA 30902
(404) 724-5461

Merchants Credit Bureau
Two Whitaker Bldg.
Savannah, GA 31401
(912) 234-8266

Hawaii

Credit Data of Hawaii, Inc.
1616 Liliha St.
Honolulu, HI 96817
(808) 537-2812

Idaho

Credit Bureau of Pocatello, Inc.
P. O. Box 1723
324 South Main
Pocatello, ID 83201
(208) 232-7393

Credit Data of Idaho, Inc.
1050 Clover Dr.
Boise, Idaho 83703
(208) 336-2330

Illinois

TRW Information Services
1699 Wall St.
Mt. Prospect, IL 60056
(312) 981-9400
(312) 763-5440 (24-Hr. Recording)

Credit Data Reports, Inc.
837 Plainfield Rd.
Joliet, IL 60435
(815) 727-0666

Maryland

TRW Information Services
5565 Sterrett Pl.
Clark Bldg., Suite 527
Columbia, MD 21044
(301) 992-3000 Baltimore
(301) 992-3055 Baltimore (24-Hr.
 Recording)
(301) 953-2360 Washington D.C.
(301) 596-4811 Washington D.C.

Massachusetts

TRW Information Services
16 Lakeside Office Park
Wakefield, MA 01880
(617) 246-2800 East Mass.
(617) 245-5150 East Mass. (24-Hr.
  Recording)
(603) 627-7583 New Hampshire
(603) 627-7433 New Hampshire
  (24-Hr. Recording)

Credit Bureau of Southeastern
  Mass., Inc.
P. O. Box 818
One Center St.
Brockton, MA 02403
(617) 588-4321

Credit Data of Central Mass.
15 Howard St.
Framingham, MA 01701
(617) 875-5266

Credit Bureau, Inc.
  of Western Mass.
145 State St., 7th Floor
Springfield, MA 01103
(413) 736-4511

Michigan

TRW Information Services
24450 Evergreen Rd.
Southfield, MI 48075
(313) 352-6450
(313) 357-5320 (24-Hr. Recording)

TRW Information Services
2675 44th St., S.W., Suite 305
Wyoming, MI 49509
(616) 532-2391

Montana

Credit Bureau of Salt Lake City
Credit Data of Montana
295 Jimmy Doolittle Rd.
Salt Lake City, UT 84116
(801) 355-5904
(801) 355-5914

Nevada

TRW Information Services
1105 South Eighth St.
Las Vegas, NV 89104
(702) 382-7031

TRW Information Services
495 Apple St., #110
Reno, NV 89502
(709) 329-3106
(702) 825-0252 (24-Hr. Recording)

Credit Bureau of Salt Lake City
Credit Information Services
295 Jimmy Doolittle Rd.
Salt Lake City, UT 84116
(801) 355-5904
(801) 355-5914

New Mexico

Credit Data of Arizona, Inc.
Credit Data of New Mexico, Inc.
2500 Louisiana N.E., Suite 419
Albuquerque, NM 87110
(505) 884-7327

Credit Bureau of Farmington
500 North Orchard
P. O. Box A
Farmington, NM 87401
(505) 325-5055

Credit Bureau of Espanola
P. O. Drawer XX
Espanola, NM 85532
(505) 753-7231

Credit Bureau of Deming
110 South Silver St.
P. O. Box 766
Deming, NM 88030
(505) 546-2793

Credit Bureau of Belen
1501 East River Rd.
P. O. Box 700
Belen, NM 87002
(505) 864-7436

Credit Bureau of Taos
Hollis Bldg., Placitas Rd.
P. O. Box 1775
Taos, NM 87571
(505) 758-4214

Credit Bureau of Los Alamos
1650 Trinity Dr.
P. O. Box 928
Los Alamos, NM 87544
(505) 662-3392

Credit Bureau of Raton
214 North Second
Raton, NM 87740
(505) 445-2751

Credit Bureau
 of Truth or Consequences
435 Main St.
P. O. Box 766
Truth or Consequences, NM 87901
(505) 894-2374

Credit Bureau of Sandoval County
905 Camino Del Pueblo
P. O. Box 11937, Alb., NM 87190
Bernalillo, NM 87004
(505) 867-3384

New York/New Jersey

TRW Information Services
Five Century Dr.
Parsippany, NJ 07054
(201) 285-4840
(212) 267-0981
(201) 285-4900 New Jersey (24-Hr.
 Recording)
(212) 233-8569 New York (24-Hr.
 Recording)

TRW Information Services
69 Delaware Ave., Suite 800
Buffalo, NY 14202
(716) 849-1266
(716) 849-1288 (24-Hr. Recording)

TRW Information Services
2450 Ridge Rd. West
Rochester, NY 14696
(716) 225-3054
(716) 225-0585 (24-Hr. Recording)

TRW Information Services
499 South Warren St., 4th Floor
Syracuse, NY 13202
(315) 474-1044
(315) 474-1048 (24-Hr. Recording)

Credit Bureau of Triple Cities, Inc.
P. O. Box 1853
Exec. Office Bldg., Rm. 216
Binghamton Plaza
Binghamton, NY 13902

Credit Bureau Associates
817 Carpenter St.
Camden, NJ 08102
(609) 963-6150
(609) 541-4292

Credit Bureau
  of Kingston-Ulster, Inc.
36 North Front St.
Kingston, NY 12401
(914) 339-4053

Central Credit Bureau
243 State St.
Schenectady, NY 72301
(518) 382-1030

Credit Bureau of Utica, Inc.
209 Elizabeth St.
Utica, NY 13501
(315) 797-1550

Ohio

The Credit Bureau, Inc.
Credit Bureau
  of Steubenville/Weirton
423 South St.
Box 70
Steubenville, OH 43952
(614) 282-5411

Oregon

TRW Information Services
9570 S.W. Barbur Blvd., Suite 311
Portland, OR 97219
(503) 245-8000
(503) 245-5415

Pennsylvania

The Credit Bureau, Inc.
908 Penn Ave.
Pittsburgh, PA 15222
(412) 288-1000
(412) 288-1166

The Credit Bureau, Inc.
1010 12th St.
P. O. Box 591, 16603
Altoona, PA 16601
(814) 944-9712

Johnstown Credit Bureau, Inc.
305-307 Bedford St.
Johnstown, PA 15901
(412) 288-1000

The Credit Bureau, Inc.
1545 West 38th St.
Erie, PA 16508
(814) 868-5466

Credit Bureau Associates
Credit Bureau Associates
 of Lehigh Valley, Inc.
531 Main St.
Bethlehem, PA 18018
(215) 865-0791

United Credit Bureau
 Services, Inc.
P. O. Box 390
Bicentennial Bldg., Suite 120
15 Public Square
Wilkes-Barre, PA 18703
(717) 824-7811
(717) 824-2877

Commercial Assoc. of Scranton
Connell Bldg., Suite 420
Scranton, PA 18503
(717) 344-7192
(717) 344-7191

Rhode Island

Credit Data of Rhode Island, Inc.
90A Jefferson Blvd.
Warwick, RI 02868
(401) 785-3440

South Carolina

Credit Data Corp.
 of South Carolina
304 Greystone Blvd.
Columbia, SC 29210
(803) 256-2600

Credit Bureau of Beaufort
604 Bladen St.
P. O. Box 386
Beaufort, SC 29902
(803) 524-4195

Associated Credit Data, Inc.
214 ½ W. Home Ave.
P. O. Box 717
Hartsville, SC 29550
(803) 332-8125

Credit Data Corp. of Greenville
304 Greystone Blvd.
P. O. Box 21159, 29111
Columbia, SC 29210
(803) 233-6275

Credit Data of Spartanburg, Inc.
126 Knollwood Dr.
P. O. Box 1051, 29304
Spartanburg, SC 29301
(802) 574-1030

Texas

Credit Data of Arizona, Inc.
P. O. Box 2070
Phoenix, AZ 85001
(609) 252-6951

Utah

Credit Bureau of Salt Lake City
295 Jimmy Doolittle Rd.
Salt Lake City, UT 84116
(801) 355-5904
(801) 355-5914

Credit Bureau of Provo
265 West 100 North
P. O. Box 90
Provo, UT 84601
(801) 373-8900

Credit Bureau of Ogden
470 24th St.
P. O. Box 1270
Ogden, UT 84402
(801) 621-4405

Credit Bureau of Logan
180 North Main St.
Logan, UT 84321
(801) 752-2660

Credit Bureau of Southern Utah
152 ½ North Main St.
P. O. Box 369
Cedar City, UT 84720
(801) 586-9441

Credit Bureau of Vernal
31 North First W.
P. O. Box 452
Vernal, UT 84078
(801) 789-3001

Credit Information Services, Inc.
295 Jimmy Doolittle Rd.
Salt Lake City, UT 84116
(801) 355-5904

Virginia

TRW Information Services
20 Koger Exec. Center, Suite 20
Norfolk, VA 23502
(804) 461-4061 Norfolk
(804) 380-8992 Peninsula

Washington

TRW Information Services
2037 152nd Ave. N.E.
Redmond, WA 98052
(206) 746-3881
(206) 746-7783

West Virgnina

The Credit Bureau, Inc.
Credit Bureau Services
278 Spruce St.
P. O. Box 625
Morgantown, WV 26504
(304) 292-7381

Credit Bureau of Wheeling
210 Laconia Blvd.
P. O. Box 6582
Wheeling, WV 26003
(304) 232-8020

Wyoming

Credit Bureau of Salt Lake City
Credit Bureau of Kemmerer
198 North Main St.
P. O. Box 71
Logan, UT 84321
(801) 752-2660

Credit Bureau of Rock Springs
507 Broadway
P. O. Box 459
Rock Springs, WY 82901
(307) 362-5635

Credit Data Wyoming
507 Broadway
P. O. Box 915
Rock Springs, WY 82901
(307) 362-5635

Credit Bureau of Carbon County
Ferguson Bldg., Suite 8
Box C
Rawlins, WY 82301
(307) 324-6693

Credit Bureau of Fremont County
140 North Seventh St.
P. O. Box R
Lander, WY 82520
(307) 332-9010

Trans Union Offices

Alabama

Merchants Credit Association
P. O. Box 10286
2119 First Ave., North
Birmingham, AL 35202
(205) 252-7121

Credit Bureau of Muscle Shoals
P. O. Box 182
Florence, AL 35630
(205) 764-7871

Credit Bureau Central
1208 West Pike St.
Hattiesburg, MS 39401
(601) 353-5271

Trans Union Credit Information
   Co.—Mobile Division
605 Bel Air Blvd.
Mobile, AL 36606
(205) 471-5387

Alabama State File
Trans Union Credit Information
   Co.—Mobile AS Divisions
605 Bel Air Blvd., Suite 523
Mobile, AL 36606
(205) 471-5387

Alaska

Credit Information
  Systems, Inc. — Alaska
14450 N.E. 29th Pl., Suite 225
Bellevue, WA 98007
(206) 883-8400

Arkansas

Credit Bureau of Ft. Smith, Inc.
P. O. Box 17077
512 Garrison Ave.
Ft. Smith, AR 72902
(501) 782-8861

Credit Bureau of Hot Springs, Inc.
P. O. Box 223
2106 Highway 70 East
Hot Springs, AR 71901
(501) 623-8833

Credit Bureau of Benton
  County, Inc.
P. O. Box 14
1039 W. Walnut
Rogers, AR 72756
(501) 636-1495

Trans Union Credit Information
  Co. — Arkansas Division
111 W. Jackson Blvd.
Chicago, IL 60604
(312) 431-5100

Trans Union Credit Information
  Co. — Central Pennsylvania
111 W. Jackson Blvd.
Chicago, IL 60604
(312) 431-5100

California

Trans Union Credit Information
  Co. — Northern California Division
2417 Mariner Square Loop
Alameda, CA 94501
(415) 521-3920

Merchants Association of Fresno
P. O. Box 1032
822 North Abby
Fresno, CA 93714
(209) 268-4031

Trans Union Credit Information
  Co. — Southern California Division
1400 N. Harbor Rd., Suite 200
Fullerton, CA 92635
(714) 738-3800

Credit Bureau of Merced County
P. O. Box 111
528 W. Main
Merced, CA 95340
(209) 722-8111

Affiliated Credit Bureau
  of Ventura County
P. O. Box 826
411 North A St.
Oxnard, CA 93030
(805) 487-3991

Credit Bureau of
  Palm Springs — Indio
P. O. Box 1357
74040 El Paseo
Palm Desert, CA 92260
(714) 346-8171

Credit Bureau Services
P. O. Box 328
399 W. Napa St.
Sonoma, CA 95476
(707) 544-2604

Credit Bureau of Tulare County
132 Valley Oaks Dr.
Visalia, CA 93277
(209) 732-6441

Colorado

Credit-Fax, Inc.
789 Sherman St., Room 410
Denver, CO 80203
(303) 830-0300

Connecticut

Credit Bureau of Connecticut
P. O. Box 1801
71 Elm St.
New Haven, CT 06510
(203) 772-3420

Delaware

Bank Credit Bureau, Inc.
P. O. Box 1884
506 W. 10th St.
Wilmington, DE 19801
(302) 429-5635

Florida

Merchants Credit Association
  of Bradenton
4301 32nd St. West, Suite D-3
Bradenton, FL 33505
(813) 753-7376

Credit Bureau of Brooksville
306 W. Broad, Suite 4
Brooksville, FL 33512
(904) 796-3547

Credit Bureau of Dade City
P. O. Box 1357
706 East Pasco Ave.
Dade City, FL 33525
(904) 567-5185

Florida State File
Trans Union Credit Information
  Co.
111 W. Jackson Blvd.
Chicago, IL 60604
(312) 431-5100

Merchants Credit Association
  of Miami
666 N. W. 36th St.
Miami, FL 33127
(305) 633-1411

Credit Bureau of Naples, Inc.
P. O. Box 7038
827 5th Ave., N.
Naples, FL 33941
(813) 262-7136

Credit Bureau of New Port Richey
& West Pasco, Inc.
P. O. Box 335
108 N. River Rd.
New Port Richey, FL 33552
(813) 849-8566

Credit Bureau of Central Florida
14 E. Washington, Suite 309
Orlando, FL 32801
(305) 843-5240

Credit Bureau of Central Florida
Orlando Region
14 E. Washington, Suite 309
Orlando, FL 32801
(305) 843-5240

Credit Bureau of Plant City, Inc.
P. O. Box Q
904 S. Collins St.
Plant City, FL 33566
(813) 752-4146

Credit Bureau of Central Florida
P. O. Box 3352
521 S. Pine St.
Sebring, FL 33870
(813) 382-3144

Credit Bureau of Greater
Tampa — Metro Bay Branch
4127 Fifth Ave. North
St. Petersburg, FL 33733
(813) 273-7787

Credit Bureau of Greater Tampa
134 South Tampa St.
Tampa, FL 33601
(813) 273-7787

Credit Bureau of Central Florida
P. O. Drawer 1233
370 Cypress Gardens
Winter Haven, FL 33880
(813) 294-3281

Idaho

Credit Information Systems
Inc. — Idaho
14450 N. E. 29th Pl., Suite 225
Bellevue, WA 98007
(206) 883-8400

Trans Union Credit Information
Co. — Southern Idaho Division
111 W. Jackson Blvd.
Chicago, IL 60604
(312) 431-5100

Illinois

Credit Bureau of Bloomington
P. O. Box 3066
103 N. Roosevelt Ave.
Bloomington, IL 61701
(309) 829-8416

Trans Union Credit Information
Co. — Chicago Division
444 N. Michigan Ave.
Chicago, IL 60611
(312) 645-6000

Western Illinois Exp.
Trans Union Credit Information
Co.
444 N. Michigan Ave.
Chicago, IL 60611
(312) 645-6000

Consumer Credit Services
P. O. Box 107
8 East Harrison
Danville, IL 61832
(217) 443-0400

Credit Bureau of Decatur
206 E. Wood St.
Decatur, IL 62525
(217) 424-1266

Credit Bureau of Northwest
Illinois, Inc.
107 South Galena Ave.
Dixon, IL 61021
(815) 284-3386

Credit Bureau of Freeport
P. O. Box 71
20 W. Main St.
Freeport, IL 61032
(815) 232-4146

Credit Bureau of Galesburg
P. O. Box 1055
54 ½ S. Kellogg St.
Galesburg, IL 61401
(309) 342-6916

Credit Bureau of
Kankakee County
P. O. Box 1789
105 E. Court St.
Kankakee, IL 60901
(815) 939-4411

Credit Bureau of Mount Vernon
P. O. Box 749
2026 Broadway
Mount Vernon, IL 63854
(618) 244-5050

Credit Bureau of Greater Peoria
109 Southwest Jefferson, Suite 200
Peoria, IL 61602
(309) 671-0500

Credit Bureau of Quincy, Inc.
228 N. 5th St.
Quincy, IL 62301
(217) 222-1500

Credit Bureau of Rockford
3917 Morsay Dr.
Rockford, IL 61107

Credit Bureau of Springfield
P. O. Box 202
825 E. Carpenter St.
Springfield, IL 62705
(217) 525-7600

Indiana

Tri-County Credit Bureau
119 N. First St.
Boonville, IN 47601
(812) 897-0116

Harrison County Credit Bureau
P. O. Box 33
425 N. Capital
Corydon, IN 47112
(812) 752-2015

Credit Bureau of Evansville
P. O. Box 8088
2120 N. Cullen Ave.
Evansville, IN 47715
(812) 473-4618

Credit Bureau of Ft. Wayne
315 W. Washington Blvd.
Ft. Wayne, IN 46802
(219) 422-6575

Indiana State File
Trans Union Credit Information
  Co. — Indiana Division
111 W. Jackson Blvd.
Chicago, IL 60604

Credit Bureau of Dubois
  County, Inc.
205 East 6th St.
P. O. Box 14
Jasper, IN 47546
(813) 482-1616

Credit Bureau of Kokomo
123 N. Buckeye, Suite 3-B
Kokomo, IN 46901
(317) 457-3261

Credit Bureau of Logansport
Masonic Temple Bldg. #7
Logansport, IN 46947
(219) 753-4161

C & D Credit Bureau
P. O. Box 341
77 1/2 N. 8th St.
Noblesville, IN 46060
(317) 773-1007

Peru Credit Exchange
P. O. Box 356
77 N. Wabash
Peru, IN 46970
(317) 473-4417

Credit Bureau of Princeton, Inc.
P. O. Box 367
403 E. Broadway
Princeton, IN 47670
(812) 385-5241

Credit Bureau of Scott County
P. O. Box 33
425 N. Capital
Corydon, IN 47112
(812) 752-2015

Kansas

Trans Union Credit Information
  Co. — Kansas City Division
Executive Center II
10895 Lowell, Suite 280
Overland Park, KS 66210
(913) 451-2310

Kentucky

Credit Bureau of Ashland
P. O. Box 1513
207 15th St.
Ashland, KY 41101
(606) 329-1100

Bluegrass Credit Bureau Services,
  Inc.
P. O. Box 156
450 Stanford Ave.
Danville, KY 40422
(606) 236-4824

Credit Bureau of Hardin County,
  Inc.
P. O. Box 885
407 N. Miles
Elizabethtown, KY 42701
(502) 737-3366

Lexington Credit Bureau
P. O. Box 934
135 West Main St.
Lexington, KY 40507

Trans Union Credit Information
  Co. — Louisville Division
455 Fourth Ave., #1233
Louisville, KY 40202
(502) 584-0121

Credit Bureau of Hopkins County
P. O. Box 307
59 N. Franklin
Madisonville, KY 42431
(502) 821-5928

Credit Bureau of Murray, Inc.
304 Maple St.
Murray, KY 42071
(502) 753-5579

Credit Bureau of Paducah
P. O. Box 2335
1646 Kentucky Ave.
Paducah, KY 42001
(502) 444-4411

Maine

Statewide Credit Services, Inc.
120 Middle St.
Portland, ME 04111
(207) 775-2109

Maryland

United Credit Bureau of America,
  Inc.
303 East Fayette St.
Baltimore, MD 21202
(301) 244-0600

Michigan

Credit Bureau of Lenawee County
P. O. Box 578
131 South Main St.
Adrian, MI 49221
(517) 263-4050

Credit Bureau of Ann Arbor
P. O. Box 624
311 North Main St.
Ann Arbor, MI 48107
(313) 665-3611

Credit Bureau of Battle Creek, Inc.
32 ½ E. Michigan Mall
Battle Creek, MI 49014
(616) 964-3777

Credit Bureau of Benton Harbor
& St. Joseph
P. O. Box 623
151 East Napier
Benton Harbor, MI 49022
(616) 926-7323

Branch County Credit Bureau
P. O. Box 70
20 S. Hanchett St.
Coldwater, MI 49036
(517) 278-2368

Trans Union Credit Information
Co. – Detroit Division
Horizon Heritage Plaza
24901 N.W. Highway
Southfield, MI 48075
(313) 827-3380

Trans Union Credit Information
Co. – Flint Division
Horizon Heritage Plaza
24901 N.W. Highway
Southfield, MI 48075
(313) 827-3380

Credit Bureau of Metro Grand
Rapids
1155 Front St. N.W.
Grand Rapids, MI 49504
(616) 456-6544

Credit Bureau of Jackson
P. O. Box 848
701 Greenwood Ave.
Jackson, MI 49204
(517) 787-4600

Mid-Michigan Data Bureau
701 Greenwood Ave.
Jackson, MI 49201
(517) 787-4610

Credit Bureau of Kalamazoo
P. O. Box 2708
810 W. Kilgore
Kalamazoo, MI 49002
(616) 343-1391

Credit Bureau of Greater Lansing,
Inc.
520 S. Washington Ave.
Lansing, MI 48933
(517) 487-6561

Credit Bureau of Monroe
P. O. Box 716
415 South Monroe
Monroe, MI 48161
(313) 241-4042

Credit Bureau of Mount Pleasant
P. O. Box 445
215 S. Main St.
Mount Pleasant, MI 48858
(517) 773-3968

Credit Bureau of Greater Muskegon
P. O. Box 205, Suite 302
Medical Arts Plaza
315 W. Clay Ave.
Muskegon, MI 49443
(616) 726-5515

Credit Bureau of St. Joseph
  County, Inc.
P. O. Box 587
111 S. Nottawa St.
Sturgis, MI 49091
(616) 651-3286

Mississippi

Credit Bureau Central
P. O. Box 1602
1208 West Pine
Hattiesburg, MS 39401
(601) 582-7181

Trans Union Credit Information
  Co. — Jackson Division
P. O. Box 221
514 S. President St.
Jackson, MS 39201
(601) 353-7361

Mississippi State File
514 S. President St.
Jackson, MS 39201
(601) 353-5153

Missouri

Trans Union Credit Information
  Co. — St. Louis Division
Merchants Leclede Bldg.
408 Olive St., Suite 600
St. Louis, MO 63102
(314) 241-4333

Montana

Credit Bureau of Billings
104 N. Broadway, Room 209
Billings, MT 59101
(406) 259-2977

Credit Bureau of Gallatin County,
  Inc.
40 E. Main, Room 2
Bozeman, MT 59715
(406) 586-5477

Credit Bureau of Butte
7 East Granite
Butte, MT 59701
(406) 723-4331

Credit Information Service
  of Great Falls
1308 12th Ave. South
Great Falls, MT 59405
(406) 751-5350

Credit Information Service
  of Helena
2501 Bellview Dr.
Helena, MT 59601
(406) 442-6272

Credit Information Service
  of Kalispell
30 E. Washington
Kalispell, MT 59901
(406) 257-7555

Montana State File
Credit Bureau of Missoula
416 Ryman Ave.
Missoula, MT 59801
(406) 728-0750

Credit Bureau of Missoula, Inc.
P. O. Box 7307
416 Ryman Ave.
Missoula, MT 59801
(406) 728-0750

Nebraska

Credit Bureau of Scottsbluff
P. O. Box 70
1712 Avenue B
Scottsbluff, NE 69361
(308) 632-2117

Nevada

Credit Bureau of Southern Nevada
P. O. Box 19060
1055 E. Tropicana
Las Vegas, NV 89119
(702) 736-2949

Trans Union Credit Information
  Co. — Reno Division
1135 Terminal Way, Suite 204A
Reno, NV 89502
(702) 322-0686

New Jersey

Trans Union Credit Information
  Co. — New Jersey Division
1 Martin Ave.
Cherry Hill, NJ 08002
(609) 665-4400

New Mexico

Credit-Fax, Inc.
789 Sherman St., Room 410
Denver, CO 80203
(303) 830-0300

New York

Credit Bureau of Canadaigua
  & Geneva
P. O. Box 391
34 Seneca St.
Geneva, NY 14456
(315) 789-6600

Credit Bureau of Ithaca
P. O. Box 391
34 Seneca St.
Geneva, NY 14456
(315) 789-6600

Trans Union Credit Information
  Co. — New York Division
95-25 Queens Blvd.
Rego Park, NY 11374
(718) 459-1800

North Dakota

Credit Bureau of Bismarck, Inc.
227 W. Broadway, Suite 5
Bismarck, ND 58501
(701) 223-7730

Credit Bureau of Minot, Inc.
P. O. Box 1426
109A S. Main
Minot, ND 58702
(701) 852-3391

Ohio

Credit Bureau of Ashtabula/
  Geaugh and Division of Credit
  Bureau Services of Northeast Ohio
1954 Hubbard Rd.
Madison, OH 44057
(216) 579-7000

Credit Bureau of Northeastern
  Ohio, Inc.
666 Euclid Ave.
Cleveland, OH 44114
(216) 579-7000

Trans Union Credit Information
  Co.
1855 Fountain Square Ct.,
  Suite 306
Columbus, OH 43224
(614) 261-3100

Trans Union Credit Information
  Co. — Dayton Division
115 E. Third St.
Dayton, OH 45402
(512) 223-6131

Credit Bureau Service
  of Northeastern Ohio, Inc.
Portage County Division
221 East Summit
Kent, OH 44240
(216) 678-4090

Credit Bureau of Lima
121 W. High St., Suite 405
Lima, OH 45802
(419) 228-3121

Credit Bureau Service
  of Northeastern Ohio, Inc.
Lorain County Division
P. O. Box 385
1710 Cooper Foster Park
Lorain, OH 44053
(216) 282-2143

Credit Bureau Service
  of Northeastern Ohio, Inc.
Canton/Massillon Division
666 Euclid Ave.
Cleveland, OH 44114
(216) 579-7000

Credit Bureau of Erie County
P. O. Box 355
809 Feick Building
158 E. Market St.
Sandusky, OH 44870
(419) 625-4231

Credit Bureau of Toledo
636 Madison, Suite 500
Toledo, OH 43604
(419) 244-1991

Credit Bureau of Warren
P. O. Box 1192
473 South St.
Warren, OH 44482
(216) 394-4100

Credit Bureau Service of Greater
 Cleveland, Inc. Wooster Division
151 South Market St.
Wooster, OH 44691
(216) 263-7539

Credit Bureau of Youngstown, Inc.
275 Federal Plaza West, Suite 902
Youngstown, OH 44503
(216) 746-5631

Oregon

Credit Bureau of Baker County
 Oregon
P. O. Box 366
1927 Washington
Baker, OR 97814
(503) 523-3619

Credit Bureau of Central Oregon
P. O. Box 1244
316 N. W. Greenwood
 Bend, OR 97701
(206) 388-1611

Credit Bureau of Jackson
 & Josephine Counties
P. O. Box 1244
316 N. W. Greenwood
Bend, OR 97701
(503) 388-1611

Basin Credit Bureau
P. O. Box 1059
131 S. 6th
Klamath Falls, OR 97601
(503) 884-8913

Credit Bureau of Union and
 Wallowa Counties
P. O. Box E
1108 J Ave.
La Grande, OR 97850
(503) 963-7177

Pendleton Credit Reporting
P. O. Box 669
320 S. E. Emigrant
Pendleton, OR 97801
(503) 276-1463

Credit Information Systems, Inc.
8305 S. E. Monterey St., Suite 212
Portland, OR 97266
(206) 659-6236

Douglas Credit Bureau
P. O. Box 958
358 S. E. Jackson
Roseburg, OR 97470
(503) 673-6661

Businessmen's Credit Bureau, Inc.
P. O. Box 3166
726 13th St. S.E.
Salem, OR 97302
(503) 364-4134

Pool Counties Credit Information
  Systems, Inc.
14450 N. E. 29th Pl., Suite 225
Bellevue, WA 98007
(206) 993-8400

Pennsylvania

Associated   Credit   Bureau
  Services, Inc.
P. O. Box 1640
739 Hamilton Mall
Allentown, PA 18101
(215) 820-6828

Credit Bureau of Erie, Inc.
P. O. Box 128
115 W. 11th St.
Erie, PA 16501
(814) 454-5221

Credit Bureau of
  Greater Harrisburg
215 North Second St.
Harrisburg, PA 17101
(717) 236-8061

Credit Bureau of Lancaster
  County, Inc.
P. O. Box 1271
218 West Orange St.
Lancaster, PA 17604
(717) 397-8144

Trans Union Credit Information
  Co. — Philadelphia Division
1211 Chestnut St.
Philadelphia, PA 19107
(215) 496-6600

Lender's Service Credit Reporting,
  Inc.
113 Technology Dr.
Pittsburgh, PA 15275
(412) 788-1170

Credit Bureau of Reading & Berks
  County
10 South 5th St.
Reading, PA 19603
(215) 375-4461

Tammac Credit Reporting, Inc.
430 Williams St.
Williamsport, PA 17701
(717) 326-0521

Credit Bureau of York, Inc.
33 South Duke St.
York, PA 17401
(717) 845-8685

Trans Union Credit Information
 Co. — Central Pennsylvania
111 W. Jackson Blvd.
Chicago, IL 60604
(312) 431-5100

South Dakota

Credit Bureau of Rapid City
717 Mt. Rushmore Rd.
Rapid City, SD 57709
(605) 342-6077

Trans Union Credit Information
 Co. — Sioux Falls Division
111 W. Jackson Blvd.
Chicago, IL 60604
(312) 431-5100

Tennessee

Trans Union Credit Information
 Co. — Western Tennessee Division
5050 Poplar Ave., Suite 526
Memphis, TN 38157
(901) 685-5353

Utah

Trans Union Credit Information
 Co. — Salt Lake City Division
302 W. 5400 South, Suite 202
Salt Lake City, UT 84107
(801) 263-8539

Washington

Credit Information Systems, Inc.
P. O. Box 70039
14450 N. E. 29th Pl., Suite 225
Bellevue, WA 98007
(206) 883-8400

Credit Information Systems, Inc.
 Vancouver
P. O. Box 70039
14450 N. E. 29th Pl., Suite 225
Bellevue, WA 98007
(206) 883-8400

Credit Data Services
1677A Second Ave.
Tumwater, WA 98502
(206) 764-6161

West Virginia

Credit Bureau of Clarksburg, Inc.
P. O. Box 1880
120 S. Second St.
Clarksburg, WV 26301
(304) 624-5623

Credit Bureau of Huntington
1015 Sixth Ave.
Huntington, WV 25701
(304) 529-2461

Central Credit Bureau, Inc.
P. O. Box C
325 6th St.
Parkersburg, WV 26102
(304) 485-4444

Tri-State Credit Exchange
901 Market St.
Wheeling WV 26003
(304) 232-2900

Trans Union Credit Information
  Co. — Charleston Division
111 W. Jackson Blvd.
Chicago, IL 60604
(312) 431-5100

Trans Union Credit Information
  Co. — West Virginia Division
111 W. Jackson Blvd.
Chicago, IL 60604
(312) 431-5100

Wisconsin

Wisconsin State File
1400 E. Washington Ave., Suite 233
Madison, WI 53703
(608) 256-6164

Northern Wisconsin State File
Credit Bureau of LaCrosse
P. O. Box 847
516 State St.
LaCrosse, WI 54601
(608) 784-5400

Northeastern Credit Bureau of
  Eau Claire, Inc.
P. O. Box 333
215 N. Barstow St.
Eau Claire, WI 54701
(715) 835-3185

Credit Bureau of Fond Du Lac
P. O. Box 969
130 E. Walnut
Green Bay, WI 54301
(414) 437-9699

Credit Data Services
P. O. Box 460
130 E. Walnut
Green Bay, WI 54301
(414) 437-9699

Credit Data Services Hancock
P. O. Box 969
130 E. Walnut
Green Bay, WI 54301
(414) 437-9699

Credit Bureau of Janesville
115 East Court St.
Janesville, WI 53545
(608) 752-5111

Credit Bureau of LaCrosse, Inc.
P . O. Box 847
516 State St.
LaCrosse, WI 54601
(608) 784-5400

Credit Bureau of
  Monroe/Platteville
P. O. Box 847
825 5th Ave. S.
LaCrosse, WI 54601
(608) 784-5400

Credit Bureau of Milwaukee
P. O. Box 1996
414 East Mason
Milwaukee, WI 53201
(414) 276-6480

Credit Bureau of Madison
1400 E. Washington Ave., Suite 233
Madison, WI 53703
(608) 256-6164

Credit Bureau of Racine
425 Main St.
Racine, WI 53403
(414) 634-6694

Credit Bureau of Wausau
P. O. Box 247
614 N. Third Ave.
Wausau, WI 54401
(715) 845-6236

Mortgage Services of Wisconsin
7612 Highway 80, 2nd Floor
Cedarburg, WI 53012
(414) 334-5111

Wyoming

Wyoming State File
Trans Union Credit Information Co.
111 W. Jackson Blvd.
Chicago, IL 60604
(312) 431-5100

Credit Information Systems
P. O. Box 1064
1750 Westland Rd.
Cheyenne, WY 82003
(307) 778-3800

Credit Information Systems
P. O. Box 1064
1750 Westland Rd.
Cheyenne, WY 82003
(307) 778-3800

Credit Bureau of Gillette
207 South Osborne
Gillette, WY 82716
(307) 682-9371

Credit Bureau of Freemont County
P. O. Box R
Lander, WY 82520
(307) 332-9010

Credit Bureau of Carbon County
P. O. Box C
Rawlins, WY 82301
(307) 324-4594

Credit Bureau of Sheridan
35 West Brundage St.
Sheridan, WY 82801
(307) 672-6424

John Avanzini was born in Paramaribo, Surinam, South America, in 1936. He was raised and educated in Texas, and received his doctorate in philosophy from Baptist Christian University, Shreveport, Louisiana. Dr. Avanzini now resides with his wife, Patricia, in Fort Worth, Texas, where he is the Director of His Image Ministries.

Dr. Avanzini's television program, "Principles of Biblical Economics," is aired five times per day, five days per week, by more than 550 television stations from coast to coast. He speaks nationally and internationally in conferences and seminars every week. His ministry is worldwide, and many of his vibrant teachings are now available in tape and book form.

Dr. Avanzini is an extraordinary teacher of the Word of God, bringing forth many of the present truths that God is using in these days to prepare the Body of Christ for His triumphant return.

To share your testimony with John Avanzini,
you may write:

John Avanzini
P. O. Box 1057
Hurst, Texas 76053

Deborah McNaughton was born in Hollywood, California, in 1950. She attended Pasadena College and now resides in Orange County, California, with her husband, Hal, and three daughters.

In 1984, Deborah founded Professional Credit Counselors. She has written and developed a business opportunity manual entitled *Credit Repair System* that has helped start over 400 offices. She has also written three other books pertaining to credit which are offered through mail order.

Deborah founded Inner-Strength International in 1990. Through her seminars she hopes to educate and encourage Christians in discovering their full potential for living in today's society. She has written a book and workbook, *Yes You Can,* to help people overcome fear, find their gifts and talents, and make their dreams a reality.

To contact Deborah McNaughton,
you may write:

Deborah McNaughton
1088 Irvine Blvd., #54
Tustin, CA 92680-3595

Yes You Can

Follow your dream
  Change your attitude
    Climb the ladder to success
      Overcome fears and doubts
        Use your God-given gifts and talents

God has a purpose for your life, and you can discover what that purpose is. This motivational, hands-on course by Deborah McNaughton includes a manual and workbook that can show you how to **find fulfillment** in what God desires for your life.

Yes You Can offers the practical and biblical teaching you need to help **set you free from fear and self-doubt** and **have a winning attitude.** Learn how to develop a plan of action that will enable you to **become the success that God intends for you to be.**

You can make your dreams a reality!

Yes You Can
by Deborah McNaughton

Manual — $25.00
Workbook (optional) — $15.00

Available from
HIS Publishing Company

FREE! Copy of *Rapid Debt-Reduction Strategies* with purchase of any $30 package below.

Package #1
2 Books: *Moving The Hand Of God;*
Powerful Principles Of Increase.
3-Tape Series: 377 scriptures on
Giving, Receiving, and God's Abundance.
Retail value $40. **You pay only $30.**

Package #2
3 Books: *The Wealth of the World;*
Stolen Property Returned; Paul's Thorn.
3-Tape Series: An edited version of *The Wealth of the World.*
Retail value $40. **You pay only $30.**

Package #3
3 Books: *Hundredfold; Always Abounding;*
Birds, Roots, Weeds and the Good Ground.
3 Tapes: *Things that Close the Windows of Heaven;*
Quality Stewardship; How to Get God's Attention.
Retail value $40. **You pay only $30.**

Package #4
2 Books: *War On Debt; Faith Extenders.*
3 Tapes: *War On Debt; The Warehouse of God's Abundance;*
Faith In God/Faith Of God.
Retail value $40. **You pay only $30.**

Package #5
5-Tape Series: *Believers' Breakthrough.*
Retail value $40. **You pay only $30.**

★★★★★ *Special Offer* ★★★★★
The Biblical Economics Library—everything on this page,
including a copy of *Rapid Debt-Reduction Strategies.*
Total of 11 books and 17 tapes—Retail value of $213.
You pay only $90.

Moving The Hand Of God
Putting Memorial Prayer To Work For You

In this book John Avanzini takes you step by step, line upon line, and precept upon precept to learn a long-neglected biblical method of prayer that will not only focus God's attention on your need, but will help bring His speedy answer. Never again will you have to wonder if your request has been forgotten. You can do as many famous Bible characters have done, and turn your most urgent prayer into a memorial that will be positioned in God's sight, awaiting His reply.

$6.95

The School of Biblical Economics,
Home Edition

This powerful series contains

- **2 textbooks —**
  - *Powerful Principles of Increase*
  - *The Wealth of the World*

- **14 tapes —**
  - *The School of Biblical Economics—* dynamic 8-tape series by John & Patricia Avanzini
  - *Giving, Receiving, and God's Abundance—* 3-tape series of scriptures to renew your mind
  - *The Wealth Transfer System—* 3-tape series reading *The Wealth of the World*

Includes a special study guide
Retail value $140.00
You pay only $70.

Order Form

Please complete this form and return it with your payment to:
HIS Publishing Co., P. O. Box 1096, Hurst, TX 76053

Qty	Description	Cost	Total
___	Yes You Can — Manual by D. McNaughton	25.00	
___	Yes You Can — Workbook by D. McNaughton	15.00	
___	Package #1 — Offer 3026	30.00	
___	Package #2 — Offer 3021	30.00	
___	Package #3 — Offer 3022	30.00	
___	Package #4 — Offer 3023	30.00	
___	Package #5 — Offer 3024	30.00	
___	The Biblical Economics Library — Offer 3027	90.00	
___	School of Biblical Economics	70.00	
___	Personal, Computerized Master Plan	25.00	
___	Moving The Hand Of God	6.95	
___	*The Financial Freedom Series:*		
___	War On Debt, Vol. I	7.95	
___	Rapid Debt-Reduction Strategies, Vol. II	12.95	
___	The Victory Book, Vol. III	14.95	
___	Have A Good Report, Vol. IV	12.95	

Subtotal _____
Add 10% to your subtotal for shipping & handling _____
Total _____

Please print to insure prompt and accurate delivery of your order.

Name_____

Address_____

City_____State_____Zip_____

Area Code & Phone_____

Make checks or money orders payable to **HIS Publishing Co.**
Phone orders, call **1-800-962-8337.**

Complete the following information for credit card orders.

Please charge my _____Visa _____MasterCard

Account #_____

Expiration Date _____/_____/_____

Signature_____